The First Family
Detail

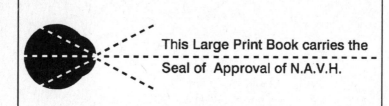

This Large Print Book carries the
Seal of Approval of N.A.V.H.

THE FIRST FAMILY DETAIL

SECRET SERVICE AGENTS REVEAL THE HIDDEN LIVES OF THE PRESIDENTS

RONALD KESSLER

THORNDIKE PRESS

A part of Gale, Cengage Learning

GALE
CENGAGE Learning®

Farmington Hills, Mich • San Francisco • New York • Waterville, Maine
Meriden, Conn • Mason, Ohio • Chicago

LIBRARY OF CONGRESS CATALOGING-IN-PUBLICATION DATA

Kessler, Ronald.
    The first family detail : secret service agents reveal the hidden lives of the presidents / by Ronald Kessler.
        pages cm — (Thorndike press large print nonfiction)
        Originally published: New York : Crown Forum, 2014.
        ISBN 978-1-4104-7519-0 (hardcover) — ISBN 1-4104-7519-0 (hardcover)
        1. United States. Secret Service—History. 2. Secret service—United States—History. 3. Presidents' spouses—Protection—United States.
        4. Children of presidents—Protection—United States. 5. Large type books.
    I. Title.
    HV8144.S43K46 2015
    973.92092'2—dc23   2014037275

Published in 2015 by arrangement with Crown Publishing Group, a division of Random House LLC, a Penguin Random House Company

Printed in the United States of America
1 2 3 4 5 6 7 19 18 17 16 15

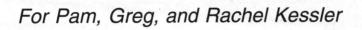

For Pam, Greg, and Rachel Kessler

CONTENTS

PROLOGUE

Chappaqua is a picturesque hamlet that recalls towns of the 1950s. Its tiny downtown center is full of mom-and-pop stores where owners greet customers by name. Here among the rolling wooded hills thirty-five miles north of Manhattan, Bill and Hillary Clinton bought a five-bedroom Dutch Colonial home for $1.7 million in 1999.

The nine thousand residents of this Westchester County town adhere to an unofficial code of conduct: When you drive past the white house on Old House Lane, don't rubberneck, slow down, or pull over to the side of the road. Protected by Secret Service agents and by a tall white security fence, sensors, and surveillance cameras, the house seems almost as secure as the White House.

With one exception.

A Secret Service agent recalls that when

he was first assigned to guard Bill Clinton at Chappaqua, a supervisor walked him around the complex, showing him all the security posts and describing how to work each one.

"At the front post, where there is a guard booth, I was instructed on what to do when a visitor drives up," the agent says. "Gather, collect, and maintain a picture form of ID, log them into the visitors' book, and make sure they're on the list to come in," he says. "If they weren't, there's someone you could call. There's a certain protocol you go down, and it was scripted with everything you do. And as I was being instructed by the supervisor, he told me, 'Except there's one that you don't log into the book: the blonde.' "

Smiling, the agent asked, "What do you mean?"

"Well, you'll know," the supervisor said. "She's maybe in her forties, attractive, blond, tan." He said she lived nearby and drove an SUV.

"When she comes in, you don't log her in," the supervisor instructed. "You don't take her ID."

Nor, he said, should the agent run her name, date of birth, and Social Security number through the criminal databases the Secret Service uses to check on arrests,

10

outstanding warrants, and other potential problems. No other exceptions were to be made, whether they were landscapers, Clinton staffers, or relatives. Only the president and vice president are exempt from such security checks.

"If we know about it ahead of time, we'll call you and let you know to open the gate for her," the supervisor said. "You don't stop her, you don't approach her, you just let her go in."

When the newly assigned agent began talking with other agents at the command post located over the Clintons' detached garage, he learned his fellow agents' unofficial code name for the woman: Energizer.

The code name beginning with "E" followed Secret Service protocol: In assigning code names to a protectee's family, the Secret Service chooses names that all start with the same letter. Thus, Bill Clinton is Eagle. When she was protected, Chelsea Clinton was Energy. As a former first lady who is protected by the Secret Service, Hillary Clinton has the code name Evergreen. During the years when Hillary was secretary of state, the Diplomatic Security Service protected her during the day, but Secret Service agents protected her at night.

An agent describes Energizer as a very attractive, gracious lady who regularly brings homemade cookies to agents. "Her figure looks great, but her bust doesn't fit the rest of her figure; it is rather endowed," the agent says. Explaining, he says, "She brought us cookies when I was up there. I was in my booth and approached the passenger door. She reached over with a plate of cookies."

"Here, Agent, I brought these for you," she said.

"She had to lean over to see me through the window and hand me the cookies, so it was very easy to see her cleavage," the agent recalls. "It was a warm day, and she was wearing a low-cut tank top, and as she leaned over, her breasts were very exposed. They appeared to be very perky and very new and full. They didn't go along with her face. There was no doubt in my mind they were enhanced."

Whenever Hillary leaves town, Energizer arrives.

"It was kind of funny," says another agent who was assigned to Chappaqua. "She [Hillary] would leave, and the mistress would arrive just a few minutes later. Obviously, someone has made a phone call."

"The mistress would show up sometimes

moments after Hillary had left," a third agent says.

"I let her in many times at the front gate," another agent says. "Normally, we held a driver's license or other form of picture ID when visitors were in the residence. The ID was kept at the main gate's guard booth we manned 24/7. Not so in her case."

"I would log in John Doe, the lawn maintenance contractor, or his staff members, and check them out, but you'll never see a record of Energizer anywhere," the first agent says. "At one point, I'm walking back from one post to the other, and former president Clinton is sitting there with Energizer, drinking lemonade on his swing right at the back of the residence. Hillary was away. It was during the week, and Energizer stayed most of the week."

If Hillary is heading back home unexpectedly, agents on her Secret Service detail notify her husband's detail so they can warn the former president.

"The bosses of each detail call each other to make sure she's gone ahead of time," a current agent says. "They warn, 'Hey, we're wheels down at LaGuardia. You've got about forty-five minutes to make sure she's gone.'"

Thus, Bill Clinton is assured that the

13

likely next Democratic presidential candidate never surprises him when he is with Energizer. A fourth agent says that on one occasion, agents assigned to Hillary neglected to give her husband's agents enough warning that she was about to arrive home when his mistress was there.

"The agents had to scramble to get Energizer out of there so there wasn't some kind of a big confrontation," he says.

Bill Clinton did not respond to a request for comment.

The duplicity goes back to when he and Hillary were in the White House. As in the movie *Dave,* they would emerge from the Marine One helicopter holding hands. Once inside the White House, they would start screaming at each other. At night, the Clintons' loud arguments could be heard throughout the White House residence.

Hillary Clinton charms audiences and often speaks of her compassion for the little people. But Secret Service agents, who provide lifetime protection for presidents and their spouses, know the real story about the nation's leaders and their families. Required to sign confidentiality agreements, they are sworn to secrecy, but they opened up for this book. What they reveal spotlights the true character of presidents and presidential candidates. In the end, that may be the deciding factor in the success or failure of a presidency. At the same time, the agents expose Secret Service corner cutting that they say endangers the lives of presidents, vice presidents, and their families.

"You can easily judge the character of others by how they treat those who can do nothing for them or to them," publisher Malcolm S. Forbes once said.

In Hillary Clinton's case, because she is so nasty to agents and hostile toward law enforcement officers and military officers in general, agents consider being assigned to her detail a form of punishment. In fact, agents say being on Hillary Clinton's detail is the worst duty assignment in the Secret Service.

1
"REGULAR JOE" BIDEN

The nuclear football is a leather-covered titanium business case that weighs forty pounds. Secured with a cipher lock, it contains a variety of secure phone capabilities and options for launching nuclear strikes that President Obama may authorize.

The president authenticates his identity with codes found on a small plastic card he carries with him. In case the president is incapacitated or dies, an identical nuclear football is assigned to Vice President Joe Biden.

Since Obama or Biden would likely have fifteen minutes or less to respond to an impending attack from a country like China, Russia, or North Korea before the United States could be wiped out by nuclear-tipped missiles, the military aide who carries the satchel is supposed to accompany the two leaders wherever they go.

When they board Air Force One or Air

Force Two, the military aide carrying the football can be seen right behind them. Staying over at hotels, the military aide sleeps in a room adjoining the president's or vice president's room. When Secret Service agents script an arrival or departure from a hotel or office building, they make sure the military aide rides the elevator with the protectee. In motorcades, the military aide travels in the vehicle right behind the president's or vice president's limo. In the event the president or vice president comes under attack during a public appearance, Secret Service agents have standing instructions to evacuate the military aide together with the protectee.

"Whoever has the duty as military aide to the president is responsible for physical custody of the football and ensuring its access to the president 24/7, within a matter of seconds," says retired Navy vice admiral John Stufflebeem, who was the military aide to President George H. W. Bush and later oversaw the top secret program himself when he was deputy director for global operations assigned to the Joint Chiefs of Staff.

But as soon as Biden — code-named Celtic — took office in January 2009, he laid down a rule: Instead of the usual retinue of at least fifteen vehicles preceded by a police escort in his motorcade, whenever he was in Delaware, where he has his longtime home, he wanted a Secret Service motorcade of two — the limousine or Suburban he rides in plus a follow-up Suburban behind him with agents.

Biden specifically ordered the Secret Service control vehicle, which holds the military aide and a doctor in case the vice president needs emergency medical treatment, to follow at least a mile behind his limousine. Also ordered to disappear from view were the spare limo, which sometimes carries the military aide and the doctor, and the Secret Service intelligence vehicle, where agents pick up local transmissions to evaluate threats and keep track of people who have been assessed as potential assassins.

Since the vice president and his wife, Jill, travel to their home in Greenville, outside of Wilmington, at least once a week, that puts the country at risk, potentially unable to retaliate against a nuclear attack whenever the second in command hits the road for a golf game at one of his favorite country clubs, a haircut at his favorite barbershop, a party, or a speaking engagement.

"When you go to any city outside Washington, you have a full-blown vice presidential motorcade much like the president's motorcade," a Secret Service agent says. "Its length may be fifteen, twenty, or more vehicles, including for staff and a counter-assault team. But when he's home in Wilmington, he has told the service — and for whatever reason Secret Service management bends over and accommodates him — that he does not want anything other than the limousine he's in and the immediate Suburban that we're in. He wants everybody else out of sight. That includes the vehicle with the military aide and the doctor."

As a result, the agent says, "You've separated vital assets from the vice president in Wilmington when he's motorcading around. We are told, 'Don't come near us, don't let us see you, the vice president doesn't want to see you.' "

Even in normal traffic, in the event of an attack, by the time the military aide caught up with Biden, it would be too late.

"If something happens and they're caught in traffic, you would lose even more precious time," an agent says. "If the vice president suffers a heart attack, the doctor would likely get there too late."

In addition to putting the country at risk when he is in Delaware, Biden insists on only two Secret Service vehicles when he vacations in places like the Hamptons.

In contrast to Biden's cavalier attitude, "When President Reagan rode his horse at his ranch, the military aide with the nuclear football was on horseback with him," says former Secret Service agent Patrick Sullivan, who was on Reagan's detail.

After President Truman ordered the release of the first atomic bomb, President Eisenhower, as a former general, recognized the need to provide the president with a mechanism for ordering an immediate nuclear retaliatory strike from any location. Under what is called the National Security System, five military aides rotate carrying the nuclear football for the president. The Air Force, the Navy, the Marines, the Army, and the Coast Guard each assign an aide. Another five military aides rotate traveling with the vice president.

When the president is in the Oval Office, the military aide with the nuclear football remains just outside, ready to rush in if the National Security System signals an alert through communications equipment contained in the football. The encrypted voice communications may be transmitted by satellite, microwave relay transmission, cell phone, land line, or shortwave radio.

21

At night, the military aide sleeps in workout clothes in an underground bunker at the White House. If an alert comes, he can rush to provide the president with the football in his bedroom at the residence. The vice president has the same arrangement at his offices in the West Wing and in the Eisenhower Executive Office Building, and at the vice president's residence on the grounds of the U.S. Naval Observatory in northwest Washington.

Only the president — or, if he has died or is incapacitated, the vice president as his constitutional successor — can order the release of nuclear weapons. The National Military Command Center provides both leaders with an authenticator card with codes that verify the president's or vice president's identity.

Because what is called the Sealed Authentication System is so highly classified, all of the information that has appeared in the press about it has been wrong. Contrary to the lore, the football itself does not operate like an ATM, with the president or vice president inserting the authenticator card and punching in launch codes to authorize a strike. Instead, along with written options, the nuclear football contains a secure phone to open up communications with the National Military Command Center at the Pentagon. During a conference call, the president or vice president reads the codes from the authenticator card to verify his identity. Military leaders and White House national security advisors then brief the president or vice president on the nature of the threat and the options for retaliating.

"As part of the conference call, the president is told how many seconds or minutes remain if the president would wish to respond, before he might not be able to do so because nuclear weapons will hit the White House or his current location," Stufflebeem says.

If the president or vice president wants to consult the written options, he may do so. If he then chooses a retaliatory option or options, his command is read back to him. When he confirms it, the command center uses the military's launch authorization codes to release nuclear missiles.

Every second counts. By the time the command center establishes communication with the president or vice president through the nuclear football, nuclear missiles from a submarine may have already wiped out New York City. While the country's ballistic missile defense system may counteract other incoming missiles, a retaliatory strike is essential to disable the enemy's military capability and prevent further strikes. That, in turn, depends on the president and vice president discharging their most important responsibility by making sure the military aide with the football is near them at all times. The Pentagon does its part by staging regular practice drills to verify that the military aide is able to execute his job of giving the president or vice president immediate access to the football.

Without the football and the appropriate codes, it "doesn't matter if we've got a thousand missiles verified inbound to the United States, we would be unable to launch a retaliatory strike," General Hugh Shelton, the former chairman of the Joint Chiefs of Staff, wrote in his book *Without Hesitation: The Odyssey of an American Warrior.* "If our survival depended on launching a preemptive strike, without the president's having [the football and authentication codes], such a strike would be impossible." He adds that it is "crucial" that they "remain within very close proximity to the president at all times."

Agents believe Biden insists on only two vehicles in his motorcade in Delaware because he wants to maintain his image back home as a regular Joe. But besides rendering the country potentially defenseless in the event of a nuclear attack, "he is making the agents vulnerable by not respecting what they need to do and making him more vulnerable in case of an attack on him," an agent says. "If the bad guy knows that they're rolling up there short and there's only two vehicles, it's easy to spot, and it's easy to take him out. He would be a sitting duck."

Thus, according to Secret Service agents, Biden seems to care more about his image than carrying out the only significant responsibility required of him as vice president: to launch retaliatory strikes in the event of a nuclear attack. That dwarfs the only duty the U.S. Constitution assigns to him — choosing whether to vote in the Senate to break a tie.

Yet despite the obvious danger to the country, no one in Secret Service management has blown the whistle on Biden.

"We drive the vehicle with the military aide," an agent says. "If the president goes down and we can't locate the military aide to take military action, that's on us. We don't have the backbone to say, 'Mr. Vice President, we can't separate the control vehicle with the military aide and the doctor from you.' "

As a result, "unfortunately what's going to happen is either you're going to have a dead vice president in Delaware or you're going to have agents killed in Delaware because Secret Service management refused to stand up to the vice president and say, 'No sir, we can't roll with this many assets short,' " an agent notes. "He wants to be Joe, and he does not want the vehicles around him. The situation is alarming, but the culture of Secret Service management is to go along, in hopes of getting a high-paying job in the private sector."

If Biden's actions are irresponsible, his behavior with agents is equally telling about his character. Unlike Hillary Clinton, Biden treats agents with respect and goes out of his way to spend time with the agents' kids when they visit the White House. Jill Biden — code-named Capri — is equally gracious with agents. But routinely, the vice president thoughtlessly decides to go to Wilmington or elsewhere without giving agents any advance notice.

"Biden or his staff continually change the schedule, and that's a grueling four years for agents to be assigned to his detail because of travel back and forth to Delaware, last-minute movement, and no set schedule," an agent says. "Sometimes he gives literally a few minutes' notice that 'Hey, we're going to Wilmington.'"

Because Biden is so unpredictable and his personal trips so frequent, the Secret Service rents more than twenty condominiums in Greenville for agents who must accompany him when he returns to his home state.

"It's tough on people's family lives and marriages," an agent says. "Because of the fluid schedule, we don't have the manpower to allow any time for firearms requalification or physical fitness training."

Behind the scenes, Biden's behavior is even more bizarre. The vice president's residence is a handsome 9,150-square-foot, three-story mansion overlooking Massachusetts Avenue NW. Complete with pool, pool house, and indoor gym, the white brick house was built in 1893 as the home of the superintendent of the Naval Observatory. In 1974, Congress turned it into the official residence of the vice president and gave it the address One Observatory Circle.

Biden's seven-thousand-square-foot home in Greenville, the hometown of many Du Pont family descendants, sits on four acres on a lake. Like the vice president's home, it has a pool. Biden also owns a small carriage house on his property, where his widowed mother, Jean, lived until she died in 2010. The Secret Service now rents it from Biden for $2,200 a month.

Agents say that, whether at the vice president's residence or at his home in Delaware, Biden has a habit of swimming in his pool nude. Female Secret Service agents find that offensive.

Because of Biden's lack of consideration as evidenced by that habit and his refusal to give agents advance notice of his trips back home, being assigned to his detail is considered the second worst assignment in the Secret Service after being assigned to protect Hillary Clinton.

"Biden likes to be revered as everyday Joe, and that's his thing," an agent says. "But the reality is no agents want to go on his detail because Biden makes agents' lives so tough."

2
HILLARY

If Joe Biden is inconsiderate with Secret Service agents, Hillary Clinton can make Richard Nixon look like Mahatma Gandhi. When in public, Hillary smiles and acts graciously. As soon as the cameras are gone, her angry personality, nastiness, and imperiousness become evident.

During the height of the Monica Lewinsky scandal, a Secret Service uniformed officer was standing post on the South Lawn when Hillary arrived by limo.

"The first lady steps out of the limo, and another uniformed officer says to her, 'Good morning, ma'am,' " a former uniformed officer recalls. "Her response to him was 'F— off.' I couldn't believe I heard it."

Everyone on her detail recalls the fate of Christopher B. Emery, a White House usher who made the mistake of returning Barbara Bush's call after she had left the White House. Emery had helped Barbara learn to use her laptop. Now the former first lady was having computer trouble. Twice, Emery helped her out. For that, Hillary Clinton fired him. Emery, the father of four, could not find another job for a year.

According to W. David Watkins, a Clinton presidential assistant in charge of administration, Hillary was also behind the mass firings of seven White House Travel Office employees. The move had been initiated by Catherine A. Cornelius, a third cousin of Bill Clinton's who wanted herself placed in charge of the Travel Office, and by Bill Clinton friends who had been seeking the travel business for themselves, according to a General Accountability Office report.

In a memorandum intended for Thomas F. McLarty, who was the White House chief of staff, Watkins wrote of the firing that "we both know that there would be hell to pay" if "we failed to take swift and decisive action in conformity with the First Lady's wishes."

When she was in the White House, "Hillary was so mistrustful and vengeful," a former agent says.

One afternoon, Hillary found a White House electrician changing a lightbulb in the residence. She yelled at him because she had ordered that all repair work was to be done while the first family was out.

"She caught the guy on a ladder doing the lightbulb," says Franette McCulloch, who was then the assistant White House pastry chef. "He was a basket case."

"We were basically told, the Clintons don't want to see you, they don't want to hear you, get out of the way," says a former Secret Service agent. "If Hillary was walking down a hall, you were supposed to hide behind drapes used as partitions. Supervisors would tell us, 'Listen, stand behind this curtain. They're coming,' or 'Just stand out of the way, don't be seen.'"

Hillary had a "standing rule that no one spoke to her when she was going from one location to another," says former FBI agent Coy Copeland. "In fact, anyone who would see her coming would just step into the first available office."

An agent working with Copeland for independent counsel Kenneth W. Starr's investigation of the Clintons' investments in the Whitewater real estate development did not know the rules: He made the mistake of addressing Hillary, saying "Good morning, Mrs. Clinton" as she passed him in a corridor of the Eisenhower Executive Office Building.

"She jumped all over him," Copeland

says. " 'How dare you? You people are just destroying my husband.' It was that vast right-wing conspiracy rant. Then she had to tack on something to the effect of 'And where do you buy your suits? Penney's?' "

For weeks, the agent told no one about the encounter. "Finally, he told me about it," Copeland says. "And he said, 'I was wearing the best suit I owned.' "

Far worse, FBI agents assigned to Starr's investigation found that, a week before White House deputy counsel Vince Foster committed suicide on July 20, 1993, by shooting himself at Fort Marcy Park along the Potomac River, Hillary had attacked and humiliated her mentor from their former Rose Law Firm in front of other White House aides.

As reported in my book *The Secrets of the FBI,* Copeland says that those who attended the meeting on health care legislation told FBI agents working for Starr that Hillary violently disagreed with a legal objection Foster raised at the meeting and ridiculed him in front of his peers. Copeland was Starr's senior investigator and read the reports of other agents working for Starr. He says Hillary then proceeded to further humiliate her friend Foster.

"Hillary put him down really, really bad

in a pretty good-size meeting," Copeland says. "She told him he didn't get the picture, and he would always be a little hick-town lawyer who was obviously not ready for the big time."

Based on what "dozens" of others who had contact with Foster after that meeting told the agents, "The put-down that she gave him in that big meeting just pushed him over the edge," Copeland says. "It was the final straw that broke the camel's back."

But what has never come out previously is that Hillary went so far as to blame Foster for all the Clintons' problems and accuse him of failing them.

"Foster was profoundly depressed, but Hillary lambasting him was the final straw because she publicly embarrassed him in front of others," says former FBI supervisory agent Jim Clemente, who was also assigned by the FBI to the Starr investigation and who probed the circumstances surrounding Foster's suicide. Speaking about the investigation for the first time, Clemente says, "Hillary blamed him for failed nominations, claimed he had not vetted them properly, and said in front of his White House colleagues, 'You're not protecting us' and 'You have failed us.' That was the final blow."

Family members, friends, and aides told FBI agents that after the meeting, Foster's behavior changed dramatically. His voice sounded strained, and he became withdrawn and preoccupied. At times, Foster would tear up. He talked of feeling trapped and told his wife, Lisa, he planned to resign.

Foster was already depressed, and no one can explain a suicide in rational terms. But the FBI investigation concluded that it was Hillary's vilification of Foster in front of other White House aides, coming on top of his depression, that triggered Foster's suicide about a week later, Copeland and Clemente both say.

Starr issued a 38,000-word report, along with a separate psychologist's report on the factors that contributed to Foster's suicide. Yet Starr never mentioned the meeting with Hillary, leaving out the fact that his own investigation had concluded that Hillary's rage had led to her friend's suicide. Why Starr chose not to reveal the critical meeting and his own investigators' findings remains a mystery.

While the Clintons claimed Starr was out to get them, Clemente says that as his staff changed, Starr vacillated between pursuing the investigation aggressively and pulling his punches. For example, the former FBI agent reveals that Starr refused to allow him to try to interview Hillary about her commodities trading. For reasons still unknown, in her first commodity trade in 1978, Hillary was allowed to order ten cattle futures contracts, which would normally cost $12,000, although she had only $1,000 in her account at the time, according to trade records the White House released.

Hillary was able to turn her initial investment into $6,300 overnight. In ten months of trading, she made nearly $100,000. She claimed she made smart trades based on information from the *Wall Street Journal.* The question, Clemente says, was why she was allowed to make investments while ignoring normal margin calls that require traders to cover any losses incurred during the course of trading.

"Starr didn't want to offend the conscience of the public by going after the first lady," Clemente says. "He said the first lady is an institution. He acted most of the time as a judge instead of as an investigating prosecutor, and then he hired attorneys who went to the other extreme."

Neither Starr nor a spokesman for Hillary Clinton had any comment.

If Hillary turned on her friend Vince Foster, she is also nasty to the little people she professes to care about. Accepting the Century Award from the New York Women's Foundation when she was secretary of state, Hillary paid tribute to institutions and individuals who convey "kindness and caring."

"All of us can perhaps find a moment in every day when a kind word can make a difference, when a supportive pat on the shoulder can really speak volumes," Hillary said. "Because in today's world, which is so complex, so stressful, people need each other more than ever."

In contrast to those comments, "Hillary was very rude to agents, and she didn't appear to like law enforcement or the military," says former Secret Service agent Lloyd Bulman. "She wouldn't go over and meet military people or police officers, as most protectees do. She was just really rude to almost everybody. She'd act like she didn't want you around, like you were beneath her."

Publicly, Hillary courted law enforcement organizations; privately she had disdain for police.

"She did not want police officers in sight," another former Secret Service agent says. "How do you explain that to the police? She did not want Secret Service protection near.

36

She wanted state troopers and local police to wear suits and stay in unmarked cars. If there were an incident, that could pose a big problem. People don't know police are in the area unless officers wear uniforms and drive police cars. If they are unaware of a police presence, people are more likely to get out of control."

"Hillary didn't like the military aides wearing their uniforms around the White House," another former agent recalls. "She asked if they would wear business suits instead. The uniform's a sign of pride, and they're proud to wear their uniform. I know that the military was actually really offended by it."

At the 2000 Democratic National Convention at the Staples Center in Los Angeles, Secret Service agents were told that the Clintons had issued instructions that agents leave their posts and, as if they were criminals, step around corners to hide as the Clintons approached.

"We were told they didn't want to see us," an agent on the detail says.

"Hillary never talked to us," says another agent who was on her detail. "Most all members of first families would talk to us and smile. She never did that."

"Hillary would cuss at Secret Service driv-

37

ers for going over bumps," former agent Jeff Crane says.

"When she's in front of the lights, she turns it on, and when the lights are off and she's away from the lights, she's a totally different person," says another agent who was on her detail. "She's very angry and sarcastic and is very hard on her staff. She yells at them and complains." For example, Hillary will complain that the hotel chosen for her by her aides is a dump. "She is a totally different person behind the scenes than what you see when she is being interviewed."

In her book *Living History,* Hillary Clinton wrote of her gratitude to the White House staff. The truth was, says a Secret Service agent, "Hillary did not speak to us. We spent years with her. She never said thank you."

Hillary's relationship with her husband is equally phony. The current location of the president is displayed by an electronic box at key offices in the White House and at the Secret Service. He is listed as POTUS, for President of the United States. Called the protectee locator, the box also shows the location of the first lady (FLOTUS), the vice president (VPOTUS), and the president's and vice president's children. If they are not in Washington, the locator box displays their current city. In addition, uniformed officers stationed at the White House update one another by radio on the location of the president and first lady within the Executive Mansion.

When the Clintons were in the White House, "it was funny, because on the radio you'd hear that she went somewhere, and then you'd hear that he went to the same location, and every time he went to her, she would go somewhere else," a former uniformed officer says.

Secret Service agents assigned at various points to guard Hillary during her Senate campaign were dismayed at how two-faced and seething with anger she was. It was the same hypocrisy she later admitted to when she said in a meeting with President Obama and then defense secretary Robert Gates, according to Gates's memoir *Duty,* that she had opposed the troop surge in Iraq for purely political reasons.

"During the listening tour, she planned 'impromptu' visits at diners and local hangouts," recalls a Secret Service agent then on her detail. "The events were all staged, and the questions were screened. She would stop off at diners. The campaign would tell them three days ahead that they were coming. They would talk to the owner and tell him to invite everyone and bring his friends. Hillary flew into rages when she thought her campaign staff had not corralled enough onlookers beforehand. Hillary had an explosive temper."

Like her husband and his White House staff, Hillary and her staff were disorganized and habitually late.

"She had children running her campaign," an agent then on her detail says. "She had a lack of organization and a lack of maturity. She could not keep a schedule." When she stayed at the houses of Democratic supporters, "We would show up at their homes at 2 A.M., and she would sleep in the master bedroom," he says.

Hillary's Senate campaign staff planned a visit to a 4-H Club in dairy farm country in upstate New York. As they approached the outdoor event and she saw people dressed in jeans and surrounded by cows, Hillary flew into a rage.

"She turned to a staffer and said, 'What the f— did we come here for? There's no money here,' " a Secret Service agent remembers.

Ironically, while Hillary is the protectee from hell, agents have nothing but praise for her daughter, Chelsea.

"In my career, Chelsea Clinton did it the

best," says an agent familiar with both her detail and the Bush twins' details. "Treated the detail right, told them what was going on, never gave problems that I knew of."

"Chelsea was always very nice to the agents, very cordial, and that's all you ever want, is to have a free flow of information so there are no surprises and you can plan for their security," former Secret Service agent William Albracht says.

"It's kind of funny, as dysfunctional as the Clintons are, Chelsea is the best," another agent says.

Hillary's staff reflects her imperiousness. According to agents, Huma Abedin, who heads Hillary's Transition Office and was her deputy chief of staff at the State Department and traveling chief of staff during her campaign for the presidency, can be just as rude and nasty as Hillary. A former agent recalls helping Abedin when she got lost driving Chelsea to the February 2008 Democratic presidential debate in Los Angeles.

"She was belligerent and angry about being late for the event," the former agent says. "No appreciation for any of it, not a thank-you or anything. That was common for her people to be rude."

At another event in Los Angeles, a female

agent challenged Abedin because she was not wearing a pin that identifies cleared aides to Secret Service agents. The agent had no idea who she was.

"You don't have the proper identification to go beyond this point," the agent told her.

"Huma basically tried to throw her weight around," a former agent says. "She tried to just force her way through and said belligerently, 'Do you know who I am?' "

That got her nowhere. Eventually, Abedin — who is married to disgraced former congressman and New York City mayoral candidate Anthony Weiner — cooperated with the agent and suggested a contact who could verify her identity.

"Huma Abedin looked down on the agents and treated them as second-class citizens," a former agent says. While agents are not supposed to carry luggage, they will do so as a courtesy if they like a female protectee, such as Lynne Cheney or Rosalynn Carter. But with Abedin, "the agents were just like, 'Hey, you're going to be like that? Well, you get your own luggage to the car. Oh, and by the way, you can carry the first lady's luggage to the car, too.' She'd have four bags, and we'd stand there and watch her and say, 'Oh, can we hold the door open for you?' "

"On TV, they will make it sound like they just really appreciated and loved those Secret Service agents and appreciate all their sacrifices and all that," a former agent says of the Clintons. "Then behind the scenes, they're like, 'I don't want to see these guys.' " He adds, "When it's convenient for them, they'll utilize the service for whatever favor they need, but otherwise, they look down upon the agents, kind of like servants."

Agents say Hillary's nastiness and contempt for them and disdain for law enforcement and the military in general continued, both when she was secretary of state and now that she is protected as a former first lady, earning her the distinction of being considered the Secret Service's most detested protectee.

"There's not an agent in the service who wants to be in Hillary's detail," a current agent says. "If agents get the nod to go to her detail, that's considered a form of punishment among the agents. She's hard to work around, she's known to snap at agents and yell at agents and dress them down to their faces, and they just have to be humble and say, 'Yes ma'am,' and walk away."

The agent adds, "Agents don't deserve

that. They're there to do a job, they're there to protect her, they'll lay their life down for hers, and there's absolutely no respect for that. And that's why agents do not want to go to her detail."

3
CLANDESTINE MOVEMENTS

When it comes to outrageous behavior, few presidents have matched Lyndon Johnson. Yet, true to its name, the Secret Service kept it all secret.

Even when his wife, Lady Bird, was at home in the White House, Johnson had what Secret Service agents called "clandestine movements" in the middle of the night to see a secretary at her home.

"Johnson would slip out of the White House for a night liaison at 11 P.M. with one agent driving," former agent Ramon Dunlap says. "He thought he was being discreet and getting away with having no protection beyond the driver, but he never got away with it." An agent would drive while Johnson's detail, unknown to LBJ, would discreetly follow.

Johnson had a sex life equal to John F. Kennedy's. In addition to one-night stands, Kennedy had several consorts within the

White House. Two of them, Priscilla Wear and Jill Cowen, were secretaries who were known as Fiddle and Faddle, respectively. They would have threesomes with Kennedy.

Wearing only T-shirts that revealed their nipples, Fiddle and Faddle were cavorting with the president one afternoon in the White House pool when Jackie decided unexpectedly to return to the White House. Her Secret Service detail warned JFK's detail, and Kennedy exited the pool, giving his Bloody Mary to Secret Service agent Anthony Sherman.

"Enjoy it, it's quite good," the president said with aplomb.

Like Johnson, JFK had long-standing affairs with his fetching secretaries. But Kennedy, unlike Johnson, won his Secret Service agents' admiration. He treated them with respect, asked about their wives or kids when they were sick, and gave them plenty of notice if he was planning a trip.

"Kennedy was genuinely concerned about people and tried to learn from them," says former agent Charles "Chuck" Taylor, who was on his detail.

Unlike Johnson, Kennedy was at least discreet about his affairs. At one point, Lady Bird caught her husband having sex with one of his secretaries on a sofa in the Oval

Office. Johnson blew up at the Secret Service for not having warned him that his wife was approaching.

According to Bill Gulley, who was then director of the White House Military Office, Johnson would spot pretty secretaries in the White House, make a play for them, and if they went to bed with him, he would transfer them to his personal staff. Of the eight secretaries around him, only three were not having sex with the president, Gulley says.

Joseph Laitin, Johnson's deputy press secretary, recalls that Johnson made a play for Laitin's secretary.

"All I know is, the next day, she was his secretary," Laitin recalls, adding that she became a member of the president's harem. "One day she said, 'Mr. President, I won't be here after next week,' " the press officer says.

"Why not?" Johnson asked.

"I'm getting married," she replied.

Winking, LBJ said, "Well, if it doesn't work out, come back."

A White House photographer claimed he always knew when another Johnson secretary had had sex with the president in the Oval Office, Laitin says.

"[The secretary] would go in to take dictation, and when she came out, the seams in her stockings were not straight the way they were when she went in," Laitin says. "The door was always closed."

On a regular basis, Johnson would sit nude in the White House pool as he dictated letters to his attractive secretaries, Dunlap remembers.

Johnson did not limit himself to women on his personal staff. He had "a stable" of women with whom he had sex, including some who stayed at the ranch when Lady Bird was there, a former agent says.

"He and Lady Bird would be in their bedroom, and he'd get up in the middle of the night and go to the other room," the former agent says. "Lady Bird knew what he was doing. One woman was a well-endowed blonde. Another was the wife of a friend of his. He had permission from her husband to have sex with her. It was amazing."

Johnson routinely closed the door to his stateroom on Air Force One and spent hours locked up with one of his pretty secretaries, even when his wife was on board, according to Air Force One steward Robert M. MacMillan and other crew members.

"Sometimes a message came in, and the radio operator could not deliver it to the old man in his room because he was fooling around," D. Patrick O'Donnell, an Air Force One flight engineer, remembers. "He could lock it. He would be in the partitioned area with some broad. Lady Bird would get up and try and get in."

Laitin recalls seeing Johnson engaged in intense conversation on Air Force One with one of the curvaceous secretaries he was known to be having sex with.

"Across the aisle was Lady Bird reading a book," Laitin says. "She was a very tolerant woman."

If Johnson had no regard for his wife's sensitivities, he had even less for his agents' feelings. On a regular basis, Johnson would tell Secret Service agents they were fired.

"Johnson told a Secret Service agent driving the limousine that he was fired because the air-conditioning in the limo quit," former agent Dunlap says.

When Johnson — code-named Volunteer — was vice president, he was late for an appointment with President Kennedy and ordered a Secret Service agent to drive up on the sidewalk to bypass traffic on the street.

"Johnson said to jump the curb and drive on the sidewalk," former agent Chuck Taylor says. "There were people on the sidewalk

49

getting out of work. I told him, 'No.' He said, 'I told you to jump the curb.' He took a newspaper and hit the agent who was driving on the head. He said, 'You're both fired.' "

In this instance, Johnson did not make good his threat. But Dunlap says the president's penchant for firing agents was a way of belittling them and was typical of his crude behavior and the way he treated everyone around him.

"If he had a bunch of congressmen and their wives on the *Sequoia,* and he wanted to take a leak off the bow of the boat, he wasn't above doing it," Dunlap says, referring to what was then the presidential yacht. "He was proud of his organ. If he had to take a leak in the Rose Garden, he did that, too, in front of reporters. They would not print anything like that or he would have their ass. He could pull their press credentials. He would sit on the toilet and talk to aides. He had no qualms about doing that. It was embarrassing to say the least."

"The first time I met him, he pissed in front of me," Johnson's deputy press secretary Laitin says. "I was a bit shocked."

Dunlap says Johnson treated Lady Bird and his daughters, Lynda Bird Johnson Robb and Luci Baines Johnson Nugent, like everyone else.

"He talked crudely to his daughters and to Lady Bird," Dunlap says. "When he started giving Lady Bird hell, she would start humming and walk away."

"Johnson would come on the plane [Air Force One], and the minute he got out of sight of the crowds, he would stand in the doorway and grin from ear to ear, and say, 'You dumb sons of bitches. I piss on all of you,' " recalls Air Force One steward Mac-Millan. "Then he stepped out of sight and began taking off his clothes. By the time he was in the stateroom, he was down to his shorts and socks. It was not uncommon for him to peel off his shorts, regardless of who was in the stateroom."

Johnson did not care if women were around.

"He was totally naked with his daughters, Lady Bird, and female secretaries," Mac-Millan says. "He was quite well endowed in his testicles. So everyone started calling him bull nuts. He found out about it. He was really upset."

"He had episodes of getting drunk," George Reedy, his press secretary, told me. "There were times where he would drink day after day. You would think this guy is an alcoholic. Then all of a sudden, it would stop. We could always see the signs when he called for a Scotch and a soda, and he would belt it down and call for another one, instead of sipping it."

Johnson's drinking only fueled his outbursts. Air Force One steward MacMillan recalls serving roast beef on the plane. Johnson blew up because the slice his aide Jack Valenti had was rare.

Johnson grabbed Valenti's tray and brought the food back to the galley.

"You two sons of bitches, look at this," he said. "This is raw. You gotta cook the meat on my airplane. Don't you serve my people raw meat. Goddamn, if you two boys serve raw meat on my airplane again, you'll both end up in Vietnam."

Johnson threw the tray with the meal upside down on the floor and stormed off.

Former agent Richard Roth remembers thinking, "If Johnson weren't president, he'd be in an insane asylum."

A champion of African-Americans, Johnson marshaled support from southern Democrats for his civil rights legislation. But his hypocrisy extended to regularly referring to blacks as "niggers." On Air Force One, Johnson was discussing his proposed civil rights bill with two governors. Explaining why it was so important to him,

MacMillan remembers that Johnson said it was simple: "I'll have them niggers voting Democratic for two hundred years."

"Johnson was in the limousine in Denver, and the microphone was on, and he didn't realize it," former agent Clark Larsen says. "They're going down the street and he said, 'Look at all those niggers driving around.' The people on the street didn't know where the voice was coming from. They were looking across the street and looking around the corner, and a couple of them were even looking to the heavens."

Secret Service agents found Lady Bird — code-named Victoria — to be the opposite of her husband: She was gracious to and respectful of agents. Former presidents receive lifetime Secret Service protection. Unless they remarry, spouses of former presidents are given lifetime protection as well. After her husband died, Lady Bird had a total of eight agents — two per shift — protecting her.

"She had a southern accent and was very well spoken," a former agent recalls. "Everything she said sounded rehearsed, because it was perfectly worded and perfectly pronounced."

Former agent Robert Rosebush remembers driving Lady Bird to a friend's house in Austin and missing a turn. Instead of correcting him, she said, "My, my. I don't think I've ever been this way before."

As first lady, Lady Bird — whose real name was Claudia — promoted environmentalism and encouraged Americans to plant wildflowers and native plants.

"Her eyes were failing, but we'd take her out and walk along certain areas at certain times of the year when the flowers were in bloom, and she'd just love to stop and look at Indian paintbrush or whatever the different flowers were, and she still knew them," a former agent says.

In August 1993, at the age of eighty, Lady Bird had a severe stroke. After that, "she could barely speak," the former agent says. "It sounded like she had a mouthful of marbles. So, from that point forward, it was never very easy to understand her, and she had to write things down, and of course, that was pretty hard to read, too. So, from that point forward, she could understand us and she could indicate yes or no, but she always had a health aide with her."

Lady Bird alternated between using a walker and a wheelchair. Secret Service agents protecting Bess Truman in her last days faced a similar situation. She spent most of her time in bed.

"Bess Truman would get up out of bed every Wednesday and go down to the beauty parlor, and she'd walk so slow and hold her arm out, and then the agent would have to put his arm on top of hers, and then they'd go really, really slow," according to former agent Lloyd Bulman. "It'd take them a long time to get out of the car, to put her in the car, take her down to the beauty shop, and she'd get out of the car, put her arm out again, and the agent would walk her into the beauty shop."

Agents were amazed that neither the Johnsons' ranch nor their home in Austin, Texas, displayed a photo of John F. Kennedy or Jackie Kennedy. Instead, they noticed a photo of the Johnsons with Ronald Reagan walking among California redwoods.

Lady Bird died on July 11, 2007, at her Austin home overlooking a lake.

"The agents knew she was going to pass, and they had an opportunity to say goodbye to her," a former agent says.

4
POTUS

Five days before President Obama was to appear at the 2013 White House Correspondents' Dinner, Secret Service advance agents began scoping out the Washington Hilton, where the April 28 talk would take place.

"The advance entails trying to know everything about the hotel from top to bottom, above it, below it, around it," says an agent who was involved in the process. "You determine what streets you need to close off, all the vulnerability points. You want to obviously meet with White House staff and try to determine where the president is going to be, where he's going to move, his footsteps, what time he arrives, the time he leaves."

Agents located a suitable room where POTUS could relax if he wanted to or if he needed to make a secure call.

"You determine where we can put him if

there's an incident in the hotel, a place that's hard, solid, strong, that we can throw him into and hunker down on top of him," the agent says.

Agents carry protective hoods known as expedient hoods, to be placed over the president's head in the event of a chemical attack.

"You need to make sure you have a couple of egress routes to the motorcade in case there's an emergency," an agent says. "A lot of logistical work goes into it, time lines, working with staff to determine guests of the president, who's going to be there, who attends."

On the day of the dinner, a technical security team began sweeping the hotel for bugging devices. Canine units swept the inside of the hotel, the parking areas, and the grounds. Including those in the motorcade, some seventy-five agents were on duty for the visit. They included counterassault teams armed with semiautomatic Stoner SR-16 rifles and flash-bang grenades for diversionary tactics. In addition, a countersniper team deployed by the Secret Service's Uniformed Division was positioned at the Hilton's side entrance, where Obama's limousine would enter the hotel's underground garage.

The countersnipers are there as observers and can respond to a distant threat with their .300 Winchester Magnum — known as Win Mag — rifles. The rifle is customized for the shooter assigned the weapon. Each team is also equipped with one Stoner SR-25 rifle.

A phalanx of Metropolitan Police officers on roaring motorcycles with flashing red and blue lights heralded the arrival of Obama's motorcade. The motorcade consisted of eighteen vehicles. They included a specialized communications van for secure telephone and video connections, a truck operated by the National Security Agency that jams radio frequencies around the presidential motorcade and monitors possible threats, and a fully loaded ambulance equipped to handle biological or chemical contaminants.

At the front of the motorcade were two identical presidential limousines. Each of the twin 2009 Cadillacs is known as the Beast. Built on a GMC truck chassis, they are armor-plated, with bulletproof glass and their own oxygen supply. The doors are eighteen inches thick, the windows five inches thick.

The Beasts are equipped with state-of-the-art encrypted communications gear and are shielded against electromagnetic pulse (EMP) weapons that an enemy could employ to disable the car's engine and knock out communications. Each car has a remote starting mechanism and a self-sealing gas tank. The vehicle can keep going even if its tires are shot out. It can take a direct hit from a bazooka or a grenade. A planned new model will have larger windows and greater visibility than the current Cadillac models, first used by President George W. Bush for his January 2005 inauguration.

Often, the first limousine in the motorcade is a decoy. The second limousine is called the spare limousine, a backup in case the first one breaks down. However, the president could actually be riding in the second limousine, or for that matter in any vehicle in the motorcade. Indeed, when a threat is perceived, the Secret Service may take the precaution of moving the president from one vehicle to another while the motorcade briefly stops under an overpass. On the night of the correspondents' dinner, Obama — code-named Renegade — and his wife, Michelle — code-named Renaissance — were in the first Beast in the motorcade.

While an agent drives the limousine with the president, a Secret Service special officer drives the spare. Referred to as an SO, a special officer takes care of duties such as managing the Secret Service's fleet of vehicles or protecting Bill Clinton's home in Chappaqua when he and Hillary are away. While special officers carry weapons, they do not have arrest authority. Regardless of the type of vehicle transporting the president, agents call it "the limo," and it is code-named Stagecoach.

As a security precaution, when not in use, both copies of the Beast are kept in the underground garage at Secret Service headquarters on H Street at Ninth Street NW in Washington. Secret Service employees clean and polish the vehicles. Any other vehicles to be included in the motorcade, such as press cars and even Secret Service Suburbans carrying agents, must undergo a sweep by canine units when they arrive at the South Lawn entrance of the White House.

On the night of the White House Correspondents' Dinner, to ensure that no unscreened vehicles got near the president, the Secret Service blocked the main entrance to the Hilton on Connecticut Avenue. Celebrities swanned onto the grounds of the Hilton after being dropped off at the curb. Only vehicles of other protectees were permitted to enter the circular driveway. But before entering, those vehicles were swept for explosives. In fact, even Secret Service vehicles driven by agents were swept.

With one exception.

Secret Service agents were shocked and disgusted to receive orders from a high-ranking agency official in New York to let in as a personal favor the unscreened vehicle of movie star Bradley Cooper. A photographer snapped a picture of the actor, who achieved fame with his roles in *The Hangover, The A-Team, The Place Beyond the Pines,* and *Silver Linings Playbook,* as he emerged from his vehicle, which was parked on the off-limits driveway.

An agent points out that Cooper's driver or anyone else who had had access to the vehicle could have loaded it with explosives or biological or chemical weapons. While Cooper arrived before Obama did, agents found the episode a stunning breach of security and flouting of the rules for a presidential visit.

"Normally when you come through that checkpoint, a canine team would inspect the vehicle," an agent says. "The canine goes around the vehicle. Your team would look underneath the vehicle and in the compartments of the vehicle and search it before it enters. Bradley Cooper was not subject to the same requirements that apply to me as an agent. I can't drive into the White House complex or the vice president's residence at the Naval Observatory without getting my own vehicle inspected. Even if it was my work truck, it would still be swept there before I drove it into the Hilton driveway. If my Secret Service vehicle has been sitting outside all night long, I don't know who's come by and loaded it with explosives."

In the case of the movie star, "somebody in Bradley Cooper's security can call the Secret Service and bypass what everybody else has to go through," the agent says. "Agents were told not to sweep the car. Just let it in and don't give Cooper any problems. Bradley Cooper had a free pass to come through the main entrance and drive right up to the front of the hotel. Everyone else, including all the celebrities, stopped on Connecticut Avenue, exited their cars, and then walked up the circular entrance into the front of the Hilton. The agents were blown away when they were told to forget everything they were told to do. And this was two weeks after the terrorist attack on our soil in Boston."

Ironically, the security breach occurred at the same hotel where John W. Hinckley Jr. shot President Reagan, press secretary

James Brady, Secret Service agent Timothy McCarthy, and D.C. police officer Thomas Delahanty on March 30, 1981.

Asked how Cooper managed to be dropped off at the White House Correspondents' Dinner in the secure restricted driveway at the entrance to the Washington Hilton, Cooper's publicist at WKT Public Relations in New York did not respond.

Obama's performance at the Hilton came off without a hitch, to much laughter and applause.

"And of course, the White House press corps is here," Obama said to the journalists and their celebrity guests, mainly from Hollywood. "I know CNN has taken some knocks lately, but the fact is, I admire their commitment to cover all sides of a story, just in case one of them happens to be accurate."

As is the case with journalists, Secret Service agents like Barack and Michelle Obama, who treat them with respect.

"Twice Obama invited agents to dinner, including a party for a relative, both at his home," says an agent who was on Obama's candidate detail.

"On the night of the Super Bowl, Obama had several guys up in his house in the Hyde Park part of Chicago," an agent says. "They made sure that we all rotated through to serve us chili."

Michelle Obama, who is protected by twenty agents, insists that agents call her by her first name.

"Michelle is friendly — she touches you," an agent says. Like Michelle, her mother, Marian Robinson, who lives with the first family in the White House and receives Secret Service protection outside the White House, goes out of her way to be friendly with agents.

One Father's Day, Michelle gave Father's Day cards to the agents who are dads to thank them for working their shift that day.

Unlike Bill Clinton, Obama makes an effort to be on time, and he usually is. If Obama is running late, Michelle gets on his case, saying he is being inconsiderate of his agents. Obama will "acknowledge you when you're there and seems appreciative and respectful to all the agents around him," a current agent notes.

As for the Obamas' children, Malia (code-named Radiance) and Sasha (code-named Rosebud): "I think they're great kids, from what I've seen," an agent says. "They are very respectable young ladies."

Still, agents have been dismayed to over-hear Michelle Obama push her husband to be more aggressive in attacking Republicans and to side with blacks in racial controversies. Examples were when Obama said Trayvon Martin, the black teenager who was shot to death in Florida, "could have been me thirty-five years ago," and when he claimed Cambridge police acted stupidly when a white police officer arrested a black Harvard professor who was being obstreperous during an investigation of a report of a possible break-in.

In listening to their talk in the presidential limousine, "Michelle's agenda goes back to when she said about her husband running for president, 'For the first time in my adult lifetime, I am really proud of my country,'" a former agent says.

But if Secret Service agents respect Obama, they say the agency's corner cutting, laxness, and undercutting of basic security protocols threaten the life of the president. The corner cutting ranges from letting people into events without magnetometer screening to not keeping up-to-date with the latest firearms, cutting the size of counterassault teams, letting agents fill out their own physical fitness test scores, and ignoring firearms requalification requirements.

While most of the corner cutting goes on

behind the scenes, symptoms of the lowering of standards emerged when Secret Service uniformed officers let party crashers Tareq and Michaele Salahi and Carlos Allen into a state dinner at the White House, even though they were not on the guest list, in November 2009. It emerged again when I broke the story in the *Washington Post* on April 14, 2012, that the Secret Service sent home agents believed to have engaged prostitutes while assigned to protect President Obama during his trip to Cartagena, Colombia, after one of the agents refused to pay a prostitute her agreed-upon fee.

Secret Service agents have learned that if they blow the whistle on such high-handed breaches of security as letting Bradley Cooper's vehicle into a secure off-limits area without screening, they will suffer retribution from management. The pressure not to rock the boat takes precedence over protecting the president from the jackal, the term agents use to refer to a potential assassin.

While Cooper arrived at the Hilton before Obama, given the orders handed down from the Secret Service official in New York, agents would have allowed the actor's vehicle to remain on the driveway at the hotel indefinitely until Obama arrived. If loaded with explosives, it could have taken out the president.

"Agents were told just let Bradley Cooper through," an agent says. "The agents did as they were told and let Cooper's vehicle through, out of fear of repercussions. That's just one example of the arrogance of senior managers in the Secret Service. They think they're accountable to no one."

5
THE STRIPPER

During his presidency, Richard Nixon maintained what was known as the Florida White House on Key Biscayne. Fronting Biscayne Bay on the Atlantic coast, the compound on Bay Lane consisted of Nixon's home, a second house used as his office, and homes for his close friends Bebe Rebozo and Robert Abplanalp. At a checkpoint on Bay Lane, the Secret Service blocked vehicles from entering the compound unless they had been cleared.

One weekend during Nixon's first term in office, Rebozo, a banker, and Abplanalp, a manufacturer of aerosol valves, drove up to the guard post in Rebozo's convertible at two in the morning.

"Both were loaded," a former agent on the Nixon detail recalls. "They had been partying. Bebe was a hell-raiser and would go on all night. They laughed and said they had to wake up the president. They had a present for him."

Just then, the agent at the post heard a noise from the trunk.

"Excuse me, I think there is something in the trunk," the agent said.

"No, no. There is nothing in the trunk," Rebozo said.

"Who is in the trunk?" the agent demanded. He told them to open it.

"There was a naked young lady in the trunk, totally naked," the former agent says. "She had a good body and was holding a bottle of champagne."

"We are going to give her to the president," Rebozo explained.

"No," the agent said firmly. The young woman had no identification. Therefore, he could not do a background check on her.

But the agent allowed Rebozo and Abplanalp to deliver the stripper to Rebozo's home. She could not go near Nixon's home, at 500 Bay Lane. And given his habits, Nixon — code-named Searchlight — likely had been asleep since 9:30 P.M.

"If he had seen the naked young lady, he probably would have had a heart attack," says another former agent who learned about the incident.

"Nixon never got a piece of tail in his life," a former agent on his detail says jokingly.

"He'd go out and have a couple drinks with Bebe and Abplanalp and start slurring his speech. Nobody would see it, but that's the only time he ever let his hair down."

In contrast to Nixon, his vice president Spiro Agnew had a number of extramarital affairs going at once. All the while, the Republican publicly proselytized about the importance of family values.

One morning in late 1969, Agnew asked his Secret Service detail of five agents to take him to a Washington hotel, now the elegant St. Regis Hotel at 923 Sixteenth Street NW.

"We took him in the back door and brought him to a room on the fourth floor," says one of the agents. "He asked us to leave him alone for three hours. The detail leader understood he was having an affair with a woman."

The agents waited for the vice president, then returned to the hotel to pick him up.

Agnew "looked embarrassed," the former agent says. "Leaving him in an unsecured location was a breach of security. As agents, it was embarrassing because we were facilitating his adultery. We felt like pimps." After that, the agent says, they couldn't look Agnew's wife in the eye.

In addition to his relationship with the

woman he saw at the hotel, Agnew was having an affair with a dark-haired, well-endowed female member of his staff. When traveling out of town, Agnew insisted that the Secret Service arrange for her to stay in a hotel room adjoining his, a former agent says. The woman was the age of one of Agnew's daughters. And an agent says Agnew also had an affair going with a blond woman in New Orleans. The agent found out because, at one point, he expressed interest in her himself. Another agent warned him that she was part of Agnew's "private stock."

Ultimately, near the end of Nixon's second term, Agnew was charged with accepting $100,000 in cash bribes. Agnew had taken the payoffs when he was Baltimore County executive in Maryland and later when he was vice president. Agnew pleaded nolo contendere and agreed to resign. He left office on October 10, 1973.

Agents considered Nixon one of the country's strangest presidents. He was notorious for walking on the beach at Key Biscayne and at his home in San Clemente, California, in a suit or sport jacket.

"He'd go out on the beach in the morning and walk by himself," a former agent says. "You almost had to feel sorry for the guy. He wouldn't know to put a bathing suit

71

on. He'd wear slacks, a jacket, and dress shoes walking along the ocean."

"Nixon could not make conversation unless it was to discuss an issue," a former agent on his detail says. "Nixon was always calculating, seeing what effect his words would have. The one exception was baseball. You dropped a baseball name or a baseball figure — bingo! But if you couldn't recite back batting averages and heights and who's on what and who got traded and who's up and down, that conversation would end just as fast as it started."

In contrast to the swagger that comes across in his taped conversations revealed during the Watergate scandal, Nixon in private seemed passive and often out of it. After spending a weekend at Camp David, the president stepped out of his cabin with his wife, Pat, to get into a Secret Service limousine that would take them to Marine One, the president's helicopter.

"Secret Service agents were at the ready to move," says one of Nixon's agents. "The agent who was driving was checking everything out, making sure the heater was properly adjusted. Nixon paused to talk to Pat. The driver accidentally honked his horn, and Nixon, thinking he was being impatient, said, 'I'll be right there.' "

While he became more depressed during Watergate, "there needs to be a new definition of depression, because that's the way Nixon was all the time," a former agent on his detail says.

As the Watergate scandal progressed, "Nixon got very paranoid," a Secret Service agent says. "He didn't know what to believe or whom to trust. He did think people were lying to him. He thought at the end everyone was lying."

As the pressure mounted, Nixon began drinking more frequently. He would down a martini or a Manhattan.

"All he could handle was one or two," a Secret Service agent says. "He wouldn't be flying high, but you could tell he wasn't in total control of himself. He would loosen up, start talking more, and smile. It was completely out of character. But he had two, and that was that. He had them every other night. But always at the end of business and in the residence. You never saw him drunk in public."

In the months leading up to the 1972 election, under the guise of being concerned about Edward M. Kennedy's safety, Nixon ordered his aide John Ehrlichman to arrange to offer Kennedy Secret Service protection as the Democrat campaigned for George

McGovern. In fact, Nixon's Oval Office recordings reveal that Nixon hoped to dig up dirt on Kennedy from the Secret Service agents he dispatched to protect him.

"I predict something more [besides Kennedy's Chappaquiddick incident that led to the drowning of Mary Jo Kopechne] is going to happen," Nixon said on the tapes. "The reason I would cover him is from a personal standpoint — you're likely to find something."

Nixon made it clear that he considered Kennedy's support of McGovern a threat to his own reelection. For that reason, protection of Ted Kennedy would end after the election. Then, said the president, "If he gets shot, it's too damn bad."

But like so many of Nixon's schemes, this attempt at scandal-mongering failed. Agents knew of Kennedy's philandering while married to his wife, Joan, but they never let on.

Like many presidents, Nixon engaged in symbolic gestures that were phony. During the 1973 oil embargo, he told the press he was flying to his San Clemente home on a United Airlines commercial flight to save fuel. He then had the military fly him back on a JetStar, which required flying the plane empty to California to pick him up.

"It was to show we were saving fuel," Air

Force One chief steward Charles Palmer recalls. "We sent the plane in [to California] empty."

Nixon often spent time with Abplanalp on his friend's island, Grand Cay in the Bahamas. Abplanalp started his company, Precision Valve Corporation, in 1949 to manufacture a new type of aerosol valve that he had invented in a machine shop in the Bronx. Aerosol technology was not new, but the metal valves on aerosol cans were unreliable and expensive to make. Abplanalp used plastic in a model that could be mass-produced. He lowered the price per valve from fifteen cents to just two and a half cents and made a fortune. When Abplanalp died in 2003, the company was producing four billion valves a year.

"Just to give you an idea of his athletic prowess — or lack of it — he [Nixon] loved to fish," a former agent says. "He'd be on the back of Abplanalp's fifty-five-foot yacht, and he would sit in this swivel seat with his fishing pole. Abplanalp's staff would bait Nixon's hook and throw the hook out. And Nixon would be just sitting there, with both hands on the pole, and he'd catch something, and the staff would reel it in for him, take the fish off, put it in the bucket. Nixon wouldn't do anything but watch."

One afternoon, Nixon was watching television at his San Clemente home, called La Casa Pacifica, while feeding dog biscuits to one of his dogs.

"Nixon took a dog biscuit and was looking at it and then takes a bite out of it," says former agent Richard Repasky, who was watching him through a window.

Even in summer, Nixon insisted on a fire in the fireplace. One evening after he had left the presidency, Nixon forgot to open the flue damper.

"The smoke backed up in the house, and two agents came running," says a former agent who was on the Nixon detail.

"Can you find him?" one of the agents asked the other.

"No, I can't find the son of a bitch," the other agent said.

From the bedroom, a voice piped up.

"Son of a bitch is here trying to find a matching pair of socks," Nixon said, apparently joking.

"Monday through Friday, Nixon would leave his home at 12:55 P.M. to play golf," Dale Wunderlich, a former agent on his detail, says. "He would insist on golfing even in pouring rain."

"When you saw him play golf, you were embarrassed for him," a former agent says.

"I mean it was awful. When the Watergate scandal came out, my initial reaction was it was impossible that he was involved in that, because he couldn't come out of a rainstorm unless somebody was with him. He was a sorry figure, really. Brilliant man, but if you set him loose by himself, out with the regular citizens in the world, I don't think he could function."

Nixon's relationship with his wife, Pat — code-named Starlight — was a distant one. Like John F. Kennedy and Jackie and Lyndon Johnson and Lady Bird, the couple slept in separate bedrooms.

On Air Force One, "Nixon kept to himself," former Air Force One steward Russ Reid says. "He stayed in his compartment, and the first lady stayed in her compartment by herself. Occasionally, they would hold hands when they were getting off the plane just for show. There was little conversation."

Pat was considerate of Secret Service agents. Instead of ordering agents around, she would ask politely, "Is it okay if we go" to a shopping center. But especially after they left the White House, Pat's drinking problem worsened. Pat drank martinis and "was in a pretty good stupor much of the time," an agent on Nixon's detail says. "She had trouble remembering things."

"One day out in San Clemente when I was out there, a friend of mine was on post, and he hears this rustling in the bushes," says another agent who was on Nixon's detail. "You had a lot of immigrants coming up on the beach, trying to get to the promised land. You never knew if anybody was going to be coming around the compound."

At that point, the other agent "cranks one in the shotgun, he goes over to where the rustling is, and it's Pat," the former agent says. "She's on her hands and knees. She's trying to find the house."

Pat "had a tough life," the agent says. "Nixon would hardly talk. The only time he enjoyed himself was when he was with his friends Bebe Rebozo and Bob Abplanalp, when they would drink together."

An agent remembers accompanying Nixon, Pat, and their two daughters during a nine-hole golf game near their home at San Clemente. During the hour and a half, "he never said a word," the former agent says. Nor would Nixon and his wife talk in Secret Service vehicles.

Eventually, Nixon gave up golf.

"Nixon was playing golf near San Clemente," a former agent recalls. "He said, 'This is a game for lazy bastards.' He quit halfway and never returned to the game."

Like most presidents, Nixon made a show of going to church or having services held in the White House.

"Going to church was more show than anything else," an agent says. "That was not unusual with most of them. It was more to give the appearance you are a good Christian. Nixon went the least of all. They [the Nixons] wouldn't go after they got out of the White House."

Throughout Nixon's career, Pat Nixon managed to hide from the public the fact that she was a smoker. She died of lung cancer in June 1993.

An agent describes Nixon's daughter Julie as "a princess, the sweetest girl you would ever want to meet in your life." On the other hand, Nixon's daughter Tricia was "a little eccentric. If she went out and shook hands, she would go nuts when she got back in the car to try to clean her hands off."

Agents could never figure out what Julie saw in her husband, David, the grandson of former president Dwight Eisenhower. While he treated agents well, they considered David Eisenhower to be the most clueless person they had ever protected. One day, the Nixons presented their son-in-law with a barbecue grill as a Christmas present.

With the Nixons inside his house, Eisenhower tried to start the grill to char some steaks. After a short time, he told Agent Wunderlich that the charcoal would not light.

"He had poured most of a bag of briquets into the pit of the grill and lit matches on top of them, but he had not used fire starter," Wunderlich says.

"Do you know anything about garage door openers?" Eisenhower asked another Secret Service agent. "I need a little help. I've had it two years, and I don't get a light. Shouldn't the light come on?"

"Maybe the lightbulb is burnt out," the agent said.

"Really?" David said.

The agent looked up. There was no bulb in the socket.

When David Eisenhower was going to George Washington University School of Law in Washington, because of increasing threats against his father-in-law, agents gave him what they call loose surveillance. One time when he came out of a class, Eisenhower drove his red Pinto to the Safeway in Georgetown.

"He parks and buys some groceries," an agent says. "A woman parks in a red Pinto nearby. He comes out in forty-five minutes and puts the groceries in the other Pinto. He spent a minute and a half to two minutes trying to start it. Meanwhile, she comes out, screams, and says, 'What are you doing in my car?' "

"This is my car," he insisted. "I just can't get it started right now."

The woman threatened to call the police. He finally got out, and she drove off.

"He was still dumbfounded," the former agent says. "He looked at us. We pointed at his car. He got in and drove off like nothing had happened. Our attitude was, this guy doesn't even know his own goddamn car."

Subsequently, Eisenhower bought a new Oldsmobile. He planned to drive it from California to Gettysburg, Pennsylvania, to see his grandmother Mamie Eisenhower. Agents remember President Eisenhower's widow, code-named Springtime, as prim and proper.

"We would say we are going to the Mamie Eisenhower Finishing School," an agent who was on her detail says. "Everything had to be correct and proper. She would never raise her voice. The car had to be driven correctly. Manners at the table had to be correct."

Afraid of flying, Mamie traveled overseas by ship. She graciously invited the wives of

81

her Secret Service detail on the trips, paying for fares.

David Eisenhower was driving the new car across the country to see her when it broke down in Phoenix. He called a local dealership, which said it would fix the car the next morning. After staying overnight in a motel, Eisenhower arrived at the dealership, where the car had been towed. The dealership told him the problem had been fixed: The car had run out of gas and needed a fill-up.

David Eisenhower again figured in a Nixon drama when the former president and Pat were having dinner at Julie and David's home in California.

"They're eating, and we're keeping an eye on them through a window," a former agent says. "All of a sudden, Nixon gets up and comes outside and says to the agents, 'Let's go. Get the car. I'm leaving.' "

"Okay, where is Mrs. Nixon?" an agent asked.

"She's not coming. She's staying."

A few days earlier, a Nixon aide had accused agents of stealing a case of wine, infuriating them. But driving back to Nixon's home in San Clemente, Nixon said triumphantly to the agents, "Well, I know who took the wine."

"Mr. President, you discovered where it

went?" an agent replied.

"Yes, David! Goddamn kid, he could've told me. He could've had it if he wanted it. He doesn't know how to ask."

"Nixon got so mad, he left," the agent says.

"Nixon was a strange guy," a former agent says. "Politics was his whole life." Despite the way he disgraced the presidency, Nixon "had his fingers on a lot more with the Republican Party than most people know," a former agent says. When Ronald Reagan was running for president, "Reagan called him just about every day," the former agent says. "Reagan wanted him to go out and support him on the campaign trail."

Nixon said it would be the "kiss of death" if he supported Reagan publicly. "But you'll have all the money you need," Nixon told Reagan. "I still control the purse strings of the Republican Party."

In 1985, Nixon dropped Secret Service protection when the press started trying to find out how much his protection cost.

"He wanted to get away from press inquiries and Freedom of Information requests," an agent on his detail says. "He said, 'It's nobody's goddamn business how much time I spend and what I do.' "

Nixon was "very private, and he hated the

press," an agent says. "He hated to divulge anything."

6
SIFTING THREATS

After the election of Barack Obama, threats against the president soared by 400 percent. Most came from racists who had no political affiliation. Many of the comments appeared on white supremacist websites.

Even before Obama decided to run, Michelle Obama told her husband of her concern that a black presidential candidate could be in jeopardy because of his race. The threats have since leveled off to about ten a day, about the same number George W. Bush received on average while in office.

The threats come in by letter, e-mail, phone, and fax. Lately, they have even been tweeted. They vow to kill the president, the first lady, or their kids.

The Secret Service investigates each threat, and if the culprit can be located, the Protective Intelligence and Assessment Division places the suspect into one of three categories. Those considered Class III threats are the most dangerous. They appear to have a serious intention of carrying out an assassination and have the means to do it. For example, they may have had firearms training.

Close to a hundred people are on the Class III list. These individuals are constantly checked on. Courts have given the Secret Service wide latitude in dealing with anyone who may be an immediate threat to the president.

"We will interview serious threats every three months and interview neighbors," an agent says. "If we feel he is really dangerous, we monitor his movements almost on a daily basis. We monitor the mail."

If the president is traveling to a city where a Class III threat lives, Secret Service agents will show up at his door before the visit. Intelligence advance agents will warn him to stay away from the president during his visit. They will ask if the individual plans to go out and, if so, what his destination is. They will then conduct surveillance of his home and follow him if he leaves.

Nothing is left to chance.

"If they aren't locked up, we go out and sit on them," former agent William Albracht says. "You usually have a rapport with these guys because you're interviewing them every quarter just to see how they're doing, what they're doing, if they are staying on their meds, or whatever. We knock on their door. We say, 'How're you doing, Freddy? President's coming to town, what are your plans?' What we always want to hear is 'I'm going to stay away.' "

"Well, guess what," an agent will say. "We're going to be sitting on you, so keep that in mind. Don't even think about going to the event that the president will be at, because we're going to be on you like a hip pocket. Where you go, we go. We're going to be in constant contact with you and know where you are the entire time. Just be advised."

John Hinckley is still considered a Class III threat. In 1982, he was found not guilty by reason of insanity in the shootings of President Reagan and three others who were with him. Since then, he has been confined to St. Elizabeth's Hospital in Washington, D.C. But Hinckley is periodically allowed to leave the psychiatric hospital to visit his mother in Williamsburg, Virginia. If he spends any time in Washington outside the hospital, his family notifies the Secret Service, and agents conduct surveillance of him.

Class II threats come from suspects whose

intentions are serious but who may not be capable of carrying out an assassination. Often, they are in jail or mental institutions.

"He may be missing an element, like a guy who honestly thinks he can kill a president and has made the threat, but he's a quadriplegic or can't formulate a plan well enough to carry it out," an agent says.

A Class I threat may be someone who blurts out in a bar a desire to kill the president, but after interviewing the suspect and investigating his or her background, the Secret Service concludes that the individual was not serious.

"You interview him, and he has absolutely no intention of carrying this threat out," an agent says. "Agents will assess him and conclude, 'Yeah, he said something stupid; yeah, he committed a federal crime. But we're not going to charge him or pursue that guy.' You just have to use your discretion and your best judgment."

In most cases, a visit from Secret Service agents is enough to make anyone think twice about carrying out a plot or making a public threat again.

Since 1917, threatening the president has been a federal crime. As later amended, the law carries a penalty of up to five years in prison and a fine of $250,000, or both. The same penalty applies to threatening the president-elect, vice president, vice president-elect, or any officer in the line of succession to become president.

Threats against the first lady and first children are evaluated in the same way as threats against the president and vice president, but the number of threats against them is far lower. When George H. W. Bush was president, the Secret Service obtained intelligence that a Colombian drug cartel had put out a hit on his family. Even though they were adults and would not normally receive protection, the Secret Service assigned agents to protect Jeb, George, Marvin, Neil, and Dorothy.

Jeb Bush remembers that when agents showed up at his house in Miami, they found the front door unlocked. "Their first recommendation was that I lock my doors," he tells me.

To most potential assassins, killing the president would be like hitting the jackpot. Often, they start off by threatening governors or members of Congress.

"We want to know about those individuals," a former agent who worked intelligence says. "Sooner or later, they will direct their attention to the president, if they can't get satisfaction with a senator or governor."

Upon hearing a threatening call, White House operators are instructed to patch in a Secret Service agent at headquarters. Opened in 1999, Secret Service headquarters is an anonymous nine-story tan brick building on H Street at Ninth Street NW in Washington. For security reasons, there are no trash cans in front of the building. An all-seeing security camera is attached below the overhang of the entrance.

Just inside is a single metal detector. No mention of the Secret Service, not even on the visitor's badge that the security officer issues. It is just when you get into the inner sanctum that you see a wall announcing that this is the United States Secret Service Memorial Building, the name given headquarters when President Clinton dedicated the building, and a reminder of the thirty-five agents, officers, and other personnel who have died in the line of duty.

Threatening calls to the White House are traced, and an agent listens in. He may take over the call, pretending to be another White House operator just helping out.

"He is waiting for the magic word [that signifies a threat to the president]," a Secret Service agent explains. "He is tracing it [the call]."

Agents try to distinguish between genuine

90

threats and speech that is a legitimate exercise of First Amendment rights.

"If you don't like the policies of the president, you can say it. That's your right," a Secret Service agent assigned to the vice president's detail says. "We're looking for those that cross the line and are threatening: 'I'm going to get you. I'm going to kill you. You deserve to die. I know who can help kill you.' Then his name is entered into the computer system."

The Forensic Services Division compares the voice on a recording of the call with voices in a database of other threat calls. No threat is ignored.

If there is a security breach or a disturbance at the White House, the Joint Operations Center on the ninth floor of headquarters can view the scene by remotely controlling surveillance cameras located outside and inside the complex. A handful of agents in the center monitor the movements of protectees, whose code names and locations are displayed on light panels on the walls of the center. An agent assigned to intelligence traveling with each protectee updates the Joint Operations Center on the protectee's location. When protectees make unexpected trips, agents refer to the new assignment as a pop-up.

Most threats come in letters rather than e-mails or phone calls. Potential assassins seem to get a great sense of satisfaction out of mailing a letter. They think that if they mail it, the president will personally read it.

If a letter is anonymous, the Secret Service's Forensic Services Division checks it for fingerprints, analyzes the handwriting and the ink, and matches the ink against 9,500 samples in what is called the International Ink Library. To make the job easier, most ink manufacturers now add identifying tags so the Secret Service can trace the ink. The characteristics of each specimen are in a digital database. Technicians try to match the ink with that of other threatening letters in an effort to trace its origin. They may scan the letter for DNA.

Sara Jane Moore, a forty-five-year-old political activist, is the only person to have carried out a plot after being listed as a potential threat. On September 22, 1975, Moore fired a .38 Smith & Wesson revolver at President Ford from forty feet away as he was leaving the St. Francis Hotel in San Francisco. At the report of the shot, Ford looked stunned. Color drained from his face, and his knees appeared to buckle.

Oliver Sipple, a disabled former U.S. Marine and Vietnam veteran, was standing next to the assailant. He pushed up Moore's arm as the gun discharged. Although Ford doubled over, the bullet flew several feet over his head. It ricocheted off the side of the hotel and slightly wounded a cabdriver in the crowd.

Secret Service agents Ron Pontius and Jack Merchant pushed Moore to the sidewalk and arrested her. As bystanders screamed, the agents shoved the uninjured president into his limousine and onto the floor, covering his body with theirs.

For more than three hours, Moore had waited for Ford outside the hotel. Wearing baggy pants and a blue raincoat, she had stood with her hands in her pockets the entire time. Agents will sometimes ask people to remove their hands from their pockets, but this time, as people milled around her, agents did not notice her.

Two days before the attempt, Moore had phoned the San Francisco police saying she had a gun and was considering a "test" of the presidential security system. The next morning, police interviewed her and confiscated her gun.

The police reported her to the Secret Service, and the night before Ford's visit, Secret Service agents interviewed her. They concluded that she did not a pose a threat

93

that would justify surveillance during Ford's visit. But the next morning, she purchased another weapon. Moore later said she took a shot at Ford because it was easy to do and she felt isolated and desperately wanted someone to take her seriously.

Seventeen days before that attempt, Charles Manson family member Lynette "Squeaky" Fromme, twenty-six, aimed a Colt .45 automatic pistol at Ford as he shook hands with spectators outside the Senator Hotel in Sacramento, California. Fromme squeezed the trigger, but while the magazine held four rounds, the chamber was empty. Secret Service agents grabbed her and her gun, and Ford was unhurt. She told her defense attorney that she had targeted Ford because she wanted to garner attention for a request for a new trial for Manson.

By definition, evaluating anyone's intentions is an inexact science. No one can predict whether an individual will commit a criminal act. But investigating threats and sending suspects to jail has undoubtedly saved the lives of presidents and other protectees.

7
PENNY-PINCHER

According to his portrayal in the press and on *Saturday Night Live,* Gerald Ford was a klutz and a dumbbell. Secret Service agents on his detail say he was neither — but he was cheap.

A University of Michigan football player who was voted most valuable player, Ford — code-named Passkey — was also an expert skier. He mocked agents who could not keep up with him. The Secret Service eventually assigned a world-class skier to his detail to accompany him down the slopes. As the president tried to catch up with him, the agent would ski backwards and wave.

"The media got their kicks out of portraying Ford as a stumblebum," says former agent Clark Larsen. "But Ford swam. He skied. He had been an athlete as a youth of some considerable reputation. The truth is the biggest stumblebum was Lyndon Johnson. He was like a country goober, falling down all the time, but the press never mentioned that, so nobody made anything of it."

While Ford seemed to be a humble man when he came into office, he discarded his old friends after entering the White House.

"The people who had been his friends — the little people — kind of weren't anymore," Larsen recalls. "His new sets of friends were the moneyed people. People who had been very close friends slipped away and were replaced by the swells."

After he left the presidency, Ford's cheapness became more evident.

"He would want his newspaper in the morning at hotels and walk to the counter," says an agent who was on his detail. "Lo and behold, he would not have any money on him. If his staff wasn't with him, he would ask agents for money."

When Ford checked in at the chic Pierre Hotel in New York, a bellboy loaded a cart with the Fords' bags and took them into their room.

"After the bellboy was through, he came out holding this one-dollar bill in front of him, swearing in Spanish," a former agent says.

At Rancho Mirage, California, where Ford

lived after leaving the White House, "you'd go to a golf course, and it's an exclusive country club, and the normal tip for a caddy is twenty-five dollars to fifty dollars," another agent says. "Ford tipped a dollar, if at all."

When Ford stayed at a Chicago hotel for an event, the host committee supplied half a dozen bottles of premium liquor for his room.

"Ford took all the goddamn bottles," a former agent says.

When Ford was in Japan for a speaking engagement, a country club there lent him a new set of Ping golf clubs to use on the course.

"At the end of the day, Ford was trying to stuff them in the back of the limo, and they were saying no sir, no," a former agent says. "And he pretended that he thought it was a gift. He started pulling stuff like that after he left the White House."

Secret Service agents say Ford never seemed to care that his wife, Betty, was in a stupor much of the time.

"We took her off Air Force One rigid as a board, carrying her down the steps," a former agent says. "I blame Ford. He always seemed to be in another world. He never saw what was right behind him and never took the time to care about her."

Betty Ford — code-named Pinafore — drank vodka, so it was difficult to tell from her breath that she had been drinking. In addition to drinking, she was addicted to prescription drugs. Because agents must be aware of possible medical problems in case they need to administer emergency aid, they consulted with the White House doctor and learned of her condition. But unlike Pat Nixon, Betty Ford overcame her addictions after an intervention spearheaded by her daughter Susan.

While she expressed anger at first, Mrs. Ford agreed to enter the Long Beach Naval Hospital's drug and alcohol rehabilitation program. There she found herself performing humble tasks like cleaning restrooms and telling her story in front of other patients. She participated in emotionally revelatory therapy sessions with other women patients.

Rather than covering up the reason for her hospitalization, she went public. With her friend Leonard Firestone, she co-founded the Betty Ford Center in Rancho Mirage. She worked to raise funds for the center, which was dedicated in October 1982, and she served as chairman until 2005.

"Betty Ford didn't just lend her name to the clinic, she was out there all the time," an agent on her detail says. "She really wanted to help others who faced what she had faced."

8
WILMINGTON SHUTTLE

Vice President Joe Biden may seek to project the image of a regular Joe, friend of the workingman, but Secret Service agents know a different Joe. That Joe champions cutting government waste while spending a million dollars since taking office on personal trips back and forth to his home in Delaware at taxpayer expense.

At least once a week, Biden takes a helicopter designated as Marine Two from the vice president's residence to Joint Base Andrews in Maryland. He then hops on Air Force Two to jet back to his home in Delaware. He returns to Washington on Air Force Two. The cost of the flights is doubled because after dropping him off in Delaware or picking him up at Andrews, the Air Force has to fly the plane empty.

"Biden leaves every Friday from Joint Base Andrews, so he gets lifts from the observatory via Marine Two to Andrews Air

Force Base, takes off via Air Force Two, lands in Delaware, and stays the weekend and then comes back on Sunday nights," says a Secret Service agent familiar with the trips.

As if taking a taxi, Biden will fly on Air Force planes from Washington to Wilmington, back to Washington, and then back to Wilmington on the same day. When the weather is warm, the vice president regularly returns from Wilmington to Andrews on an airplane on Saturdays to play golf at the Air Force base with President Obama. After the five-hour golf game, he flies back to New Castle Airport in Wilmington — all at taxpayer expense.

"Every three or four weeks when it's warm, Biden gets up there on Saturday and then will fly back on Air Force Two," says a Secret Service agent. "While Air Force Two is sitting on the tarmac at Andrews, he goes and plays golf with the president at Andrews Air Force Base, gets back on the plane, and flies back to Delaware. Let me tell you something, that is egregious."

Besides that, "The Secret Service rents condos in Wilmington because his schedule is so fluid and never concrete enough to properly prepare for his visits to Delaware," the agent says. "So they keep a fully staffed

Secret Service advance team in Delaware in condominiums that we lease so that when he does these things back and forth to D.C., they're up there ready for him to arrive."

Until now, Biden has managed to keep the details of his personal trips and the costs a secret. Seeking to get the answers, I filed a Freedom of Information (FOIA) request with the Air Force in April 2013. Having received no response three months later, I looked into it and learned from Air Force sources what had happened behind the scenes: Air Force FOIA officers had done their jobs and within a few weeks of my request had compiled the information, including the dates of Biden's trips, empty so-called deadhead trips to pick him up or leave him off, and the actual costs by type of aircraft.

But in what amounts to a cover-up on behalf of the vice president, on June 6, Biden's office blocked transmitting the results to me and told Air Force officers they were not to comment to anyone about the case.

Instead, in an e-mail to the Air Force chief of Special Air Missions — which arranges flights for Obama, Biden, Cabinet officers, members of Congress, and foreign dignitaries — Jessica R. Hertz, who is Biden's deputy counsel in his Senate office, expressed a series of "concerns" about the FOIA request and claimed she did not fully understand what I was requesting.

Hertz has no trouble understanding the English language: In 2007 and 2008, she was a U.S. Court of Appeals clerk to Judge Sonia Sotomayor before President Obama nominated her to the Supreme Court. In 2009, Sotomayor officiated at Hertz's wedding at the Metropolitan Club in New York.

Hertz placed herself in charge of the FOIA case and, on the grounds that they were not "source documents," ordered Air Force FOIA officers not to give me the ninety-five pages of records they had already compiled in response to my request. Rather, she instructed, to retrieve the flight data, Air Force officers must examine individual logs of each aircraft Biden flew on going back to January 2009, when he took office.

To make the release of the data even less likely, Hertz told the chief of Special Air Missions that the Secret Service would have to be consulted before any data would be provided to me. In addition, any official statement about the case would have to come from Biden's office, she told the Air Force in an e-mail.

Calling Hertz's claims "ridiculous," an Air

Force officer familiar with the matter said the data compiled in response to the FOIA request were the Air Force's computer records that come directly from aircraft flight logs.

"They are covering up," the Air Force officer said. "We spent a lot of time compiling the records, but Biden's office said logs for each flight would have to be consulted. This is a smokescreen designed to delay providing any records as long as possible."

Contrary to Hertz's claim to the Air Force that individual flight logs must be examined, the Freedom of Information Act requires the government to provide access to existing "records," which specifically include electronic computerized records. The act says nothing about "source documents." Moreover, nonpolitical government employees are supposed to process FOIA requests, releasing documents regardless of whether they may embarrass the brass. In this case, the brass took over.

After hearing from Hertz, the Pentagon transferred the FOIA request to the Air Mobility Command, which includes the 89th Airlift Wing, the Air Force component responsible for Air Force One and Air Force Two. Regardless of which plane is used, aircraft carrying the president are identified with the call sign Air Force One, while flights transporting the vice president are designated Air Force Two. The command told me a response to the FOIA request would be delayed because of the "high-level coordination required on these types of records."

The attempt by the vice president's office to suppress results already compiled appears to be unprecedented and conflicts with Obama's directive to agencies to "apply a presumption of openness in responding to FOIA requests." Much like President Nixon's cover-ups, it is an effort to direct government officials to hide personal abuse.

Despite the cover-up, shortly after Hertz intervened, an Air Force officer provided me with the records compiled in response to the FOIA request that Hertz claimed she did not understand. The officer was outraged that Biden's office would taint the Air Force by politicizing its FOIA process. Without telling her that I had already received the records in question, I e-mailed Hertz to ask what she did not understand about my request. She did not respond.

The Air Force records show that from the time Biden took office in January 2009 until March 2013, the vice president's trips back and forth between Andrews and Wilmington cost taxpayers $979,680 for fuel and maintenance. That figure does not include the additional costs of flying Biden on the Marine Two helicopter to and from the vice president's residence at the Naval Observatory and Andrews. Nor does it include crew costs for his frequent trips.

In fiscal year 2012, the cost to taxpayers for Biden's Air Force Two flights alone amounted to $288,080, including deadhead trips. The flights totaled 62.8 hours on a C-32, which is the military version of the Boeing 757-200; on a C-40B, which is a Boeing 737-700; and on a C-20B, C-37A, or C-37B, which are Gulfstream aircraft.

The records show Biden thinks nothing of flying back and forth to Wilmington multiple times on the same day. For example, on Friday, February 8, 2013, Biden flew from Andrews to Wilmington and back to Andrews on a C-37A, then returned that same day to Wilmington on a C-20B. Since deadhead flights were required to pick him up or drop him off, that taxi service entailed four flights in one day at taxpayer expense.

In some cases, because Biden must be on a flight before the Air Force will pay for it, he has flown from Andrews to Wilmington to pick up his wife, Jill, then immediately flown back with her to Washington, according to an Air Force source who arranges his flights. In addition, according to an Air Force source, Biden regularly schedules a single public event in Arizona so he can fly there on Air Force Two at government expense with his family to play golf.

Biden's use of Air Force assets to play golf with President Obama is even more egregious. For example, on Saturday, April 21, 2012, Biden flew from Wilmington to Andrews to play golf with Obama, White House trip director Marvin Nicholson, and White House staffer Mike Brush.

Biden then flew back to Wilmington, requiring two deadhead flights. Including the deadhead trips, the cost to taxpayers for that one golfing outing back and forth on a C-20B was $12,406. Since Air Force Two parks at Andrews for these games, Obama is obviously aware that Biden is running up a colossal government tab for each game of golf he plays with him.

More than six months after Biden's counsel Hertz intervened, an Air Mobility Command Freedom of Information Act officer responded to my FOIA request and provided the records of Biden's trips that Hertz had tried to suppress. They confirm that between March 2009 and March 2013, Biden flew to Wilmington or flew back to

Washington two hundred twenty-five times. The personal trips required a total of four hundred flights, including deadhead trips.

Biden's press office had no comment on his trips.

In view of his trips, Secret Service agents on Biden's detail chuckled when Obama announced in 2011 that he was placing Biden in charge of a Campaign to Cut Waste that was supposed to root out unnecessary government spending. In making the announcement, Obama said Biden would "hunt down and eliminate misspent tax dollars in every agency and department across the federal government."

In an e-mail to supporters, Biden proclaimed himself the "new sheriff in town." He said that "particularly at a time when we're facing tough decisions about reducing our deficit, it's a no-brainer to stop spending taxpayer dollars on things that benefit nobody."

Yet besides spending a million dollars on personal trips to Delaware and receiving an annual salary of $230,700 as vice president, Biden has free use of the vice president's residence on the grounds of the U.S. Naval Observatory. At least five Navy stewards attend to every personal need of Biden and Jill, including cooking, shopping for food, cleaning, and doing the laundry.

As a U.S. senator, Biden proudly publicized the fact that he commuted daily by train from his home in Delaware to Washington during the week. Amtrak named the newly renovated Wilmington station the Joseph R. Biden Jr. Railroad Station. But after taking office as vice president, a Secret Service agent says Biden began the pattern of commuting to his Delaware home on Air Force Two.

While Secret Service agents say flying is the most secure way for Biden to make the trips, the question is why the sheriff who is supposed to cut out government waste thinks it is appropriate to take such frequent trips for personal reasons, even flying back and forth to Andrews on the same day to play golf with Obama. They note that Biden has continued the trips despite the fact that government employees have seen their salaries cut because of the sequester and its budget reductions.

Among themselves, Secret Service agents assigned to Biden's detail and officers of the 89th Airlift Wing, which flies the planes, express outrage at what they consider an abuse. Given the fact that Biden's job is in Washington, where the government provides him with a luxurious mansion, they say there is no justification for charging the government for such frequent trips back home. They refer derisively to Biden's practice of constantly flying back and forth as the "Wilmington shuttle."

"The Air Force Two guys pull their hair out over this," says a Secret Service agent who deals with the crew. In contrast to Biden, Obama reserves personal trips on Air Force One for occasional vacations, Air Force officers point out.

While agents personally like the potential 2016 presidential candidate, "that doesn't mean we don't see the waste, abuse, and risk-taking," a current agent says, referring to Biden's insistence that his aide with the nuclear football remain separated from his motorcade in Delaware.

9

ADVANCE

Today the President's Protective Detail consists of three hundred agents, including those protecting the president's family, and assigns twenty-five to forty agents to the president per shift. The Vice President's Protective Detail consists of one hundred fifty agents. In all, the Secret Service has thirty-five hundred special agents, compared with three hundred in John F. Kennedy's day.

As the president moves about in public, six agents surround him. They include a shift supervisor and a detail leader.

"The detail leader is right on him or very close," an agent says. "He's literally right behind him, probably with his hand on his back or maybe even holding on to his belt, so that if he had to pull him or pivot him, he could do that right away."

When the president is advancing, the agents form a box configuration, and if he's moving down a narrow corridor, they form a diamond configuration. Other agents stand post at access points.

After 9/11, President Bush roughly doubled the number of individuals given Secret Service protection to twenty-seven permanent protectees, plus ten family members. Another seven were protected when traveling abroad. President Obama has increased the number under protection to forty-five, including aides such as Valerie Jarrett.

When Kennedy was president, the Secret Service conducted little advance work before a presidential visit. Today, ten days before a presidential visit out of town, the Secret Service dispatches eight to ten agents to conduct advance planning.

An advance team includes a lead agent, a transportation agent, an airport agent, agents assigned to each event site, a hotel advance agent, one or two logistics agents, a technical security agent, and an intelligence agent. As part of advance preparations, a team of military communications personnel from the Defense Department's White House Communications Agency is dispatched to handle radios and phones. They ship their equipment and additional personnel on Air Force C-130 cargo planes. Depending on how much exposure the president will encounter, members of the Uniformed Division's countersniper team and the counterassault team from the Secret Service's Special Operations Division may go along on an advance.

Before the president is checked in, an entire floor of a hotel is reserved, plus the two floors below. Agents sweep the area for explosives, bugging devices, and radioactive material or other contaminants. They check carpeting for concealed objects. They examine picture frames that could be hollow and conceal explosives. They install bulletproof glass on windows, and they plan escape routes from every room that the president might enter.

"In the hotel, if the president will stay overnight, we secure the suite and floor he will stay on and make it as safe as the White House," an agent says. "We seal it off. No other guests can be on the floor. If the floor is huge, we will separate it [with guarded partitions]. But no outside people will be on the floor, guaranteed."

The Secret Service checks the backgrounds of employees who prepare food for the president and other members of the first family during a trip. If an employee has been convicted of an assault or drug violation, agents will ask the dining establishment to give the employee a day off. To ensure that no one slips poison into food served the president at a hotel or restaurant, an agent randomly selects from the prepared dishes the one to be served to the president and watches as it is brought out to him. Employees who have been cleared are given color-coded pins to wear. On overseas trips, Navy stewards might prepare dishes for the president. With food prepared at the White House, the Secret Service is not directly involved.

"You can't watch everything," a Secret Service agent says. "But the majority of stuff is checked. We have lists of the suppliers. We check the employees once and go back randomly and check them again to see if anyone has been added."

In contrast to the cursory look the Secret Service gave to John F. Kennedy's planned Dallas parade route, its Forensic Services Division now creates virtual three-dimensional models of buildings along a motorcade route so that agents will know what to expect and can plan what to do at spots where the motorcade may be more vulnerable to attack. The division also produces slide shows of the floor plans of buildings where the president will speak.

"We're doing things now that are so much more advanced than what they would have done before 9/11," an agent says. "The work that we do now is just so much more comprehensive and detailed."

During the advance for a presidential trip, the Secret Service picks out safe houses, such as fire stations, to be used in case of a threat. It plots the best routes to local hospitals and alerts the hospitals of an impending presidential visit.

As many as twenty-five vehicles could comprise the president's motorcade. A helicopter hovers overhead, and no aircraft are allowed in the area.

For an overseas trip, military cargo planes airlift in more than fifty support vehicles. Fighter jets fly overhead so they can intervene quickly if a plane gets too close to the president's location on the ground. As many as six hundred people could be included on an overseas presidential trip, including military personnel and up to fifty Secret Service agents. Including the White House doctor and other administration personnel, a domestic presidential trip entails two hundred to three hundred people.

Back in Washington, advance work for an inauguration is even more elaborate. The Secret Service canvasses the area along the parade route and spot-welds shut manhole covers and removes trash cans and mailboxes. If an item like a utility vault cannot be removed, it is inspected and taped shut. If anyone tampers with the special tape — color-coded for each event — it disintegrates to warn agents that someone may have gained access to a secured area.

Concrete barriers or police cars block every street in Washington leading to the motorcade route. Spectators must pass through magnetometers before entering the area of the motorcade route. Coolers, backpacks, and packages are banned.

Bomb-sniffing dogs inspect buildings, garages, and delivery trucks. Employees in offices and hotel guests along the route are often checked for criminal records. Agents make sure they have access to every office and hotel room, with master keys from the building or hotel manager. They tape shut utility rooms and electrical circuit boards along the parade route.

Agents or police officers are stationed on roofs of buildings. More than a dozen countersniper teams are deployed at the most vulnerable points. High-resolution surveillance cameras scan the crowds.

"Every window must be closed when the motorcade passes," a supervisory agent says.

"We have spotters looking at them with binoculars. For the most part they comply. If they don't, we have master keys to all those doors. We ask them why they are there and opening the windows."

The Secret Service scripts exactly where the president and first lady are to step out of the Beast and wave to crowds following the inauguration. Counterassault teams armed with semiautomatic Stoner SR-16 rifles and flash-bang grenades for diversionary tactics are positioned at these critical points.

If agents encounter a problem, they call for an ID team. Named for the Intelligence Division, the ID team at an event is usually composed of a Secret Service agent and a local police officer. Upon learning of a potential threat, the team races to the scene, interviews the subject, takes control of the situation, and passes along any threat information to the detail.

Protection of the first lady and first kids outside the White House is essentially the same as protecting the president and vice president, except that fewer agents are assigned. Depending on the type of venue, as many as thirty-five to forty agents may accompany the president when he leaves the White House, compared to four to six agents for the first lady and three to four for a first child.

As with the president and vice president, agents allow the first lady and first kids a comfort zone: Agents do not sit in on classrooms, for example, but will station themselves around a school and down the corridor from a classroom. In the same way, agents are not stationed in the residence portion of the White House. However, as with the president and vice president, agents accompany the first lady and first kids wherever they go — to soccer practice, to friends' houses, and to vacation spots.

If a president's child is going to a birthday party in a private home, agents check out the house beforehand. Given that the host vouches for the young guests by inviting them, agents will not screen them with magnetometers or conduct background checks. During the party, agents station themselves in an adjoining room or in the basement and sit outside in Suburbans. If an event is an "off-the-record movement" where no one knows that the president's children will be attending, agents likely will not check out the premises beforehand.

Where the children go to school is the decision of the president and first lady, and often they send the kids to private schools, where security may be tighter. Jimmy and Rosalynn Carter made a political statement by sending Amy to a public school in northwest Washington called Hardy Middle School.

Most of the time, Secret Service agents had little more to contend with than sixth-grade boys speculating on how they would tie together an agent's shoelaces were he to fall asleep under the tree where he sat watching Amy play soccer at recess. But at one point, the Secret Service received intelligence that Middle Eastern terrorists might be planning to try to kidnap Amy.

"We put in a counterassault team," says former agent Dennis Chomicki, who was a member of the team. "We had five armed guys hanging around with some pretty heavy weapons. We did it for weeks until we felt it was not going to happen."

For agents, the path to protecting the first family begins in a field office. Agents in field offices spend most of their time investigating financial crimes — counterfeiting, check fraud, access-device fraud, identity theft, and computer-based attacks on the nation's financial, banking, and telecommunications infrastructure. But when the president, the vice president, or a presidential candidate visits their city, agents in the field are often assigned to protective duties. If a threat requires investigation in their city, they will follow leads and conduct the necessary interviews.

Typically after seven years in one or more field offices, agents may be assigned to the President's Protective Detail (PPD) or to the Vice President's Protective Detail (VPD), where they usually serve for the duration of the president's or vice president's four-year term. Alternatively, they may be assigned to the Technical Services Division, the Protective Intelligence and Assessment Division, the Dignitary Protection Division, the Financial Crimes Division, or to the protection of former presidents and their spouses. After about six months, agents may be assigned to protect the president's or vice president's wife or children. These are called satellite details of the PPD or VPD.

While the president's detail may seem more prestigious than the vice president's, "I've never seen anybody say anything bad because you're on VPD or considered a lesser agent," a current agent says. "I think there's a certain arrogance that agents have, considering what they do, but I wouldn't say that there's a rivalry."

After another six months, agents may

return to the PPD or the VPD or may be assigned to drive the presidential or vice presidential limousine or to return to one of the specialty divisions. Finally, after three to five years in this phase of their careers, agents return to a field office or are promoted to a job in headquarters.

Not including overtime, an experienced agent makes $110,000 a year, including a cost-of-living adjustment for Washington. After twenty years of service, agents can retire at age fifty with a pension of 34 percent of the average of their three highest-paid years. Agents may also retire at any age with twenty-five years of service.

While threats aimed at first family members like Michelle Obama and her kids come in routinely, the number is minimal compared with those aimed at the president. Still, agents worry just as much about threats against the family as about those against the president, recognizing that a president's wife or children could be targets or taken hostage at any time.

In conducting an advance before an inauguration or a trip, agents consult with local law enforcement. In one of the more bizarre events in Secret Service history, when President George H. W. Bush was to give a speech in Enid, Oklahoma, on September

17, 1992, local law enforcement officials told agents that a resident who was a psychic had had a vision that a sniper on an overpass would shoot Bush. The authorities said the psychic had been incredibly reliable in the past, even leading police to the bodies of murder victims and providing useful leads in other cases.

Norm Jarvis, who was assigned to run intelligence investigations for the visit, remembered seeing the psychic, Patsy Jane Henigman, on television. Sporting a beehive hairdo, she would don what she called a special pair of cowboy boots and then tell police not only where bodies were buried but how the victims had been murdered.

The evening before Bush's visit, Jarvis and his partner drove to Henigman's home in Enid.

"While it may seem surprising that the Secret Service would pay attention to a self-proclaimed psychic, we talk to them, not because they may have psychic powers, but to try and determine if they have legitimately picked up information from someone about an assassination plot or have access to sensitive insider information," Jarvis says.

Henigman invited them in, and Jarvis explained why they were there. The psychic confirmed that she had had a vision that the president was about to be assassinated.

Jarvis asked Henigman to describe her vision. The woman said she saw the president arriving in Oklahoma: He gets off the plane, and he gets in a limousine and sits behind the driver. When Bush gets in his limousine, he is not wearing a suit. Instead, he is wearing a light jacket and an open-collar shirt. According to her vision, as they start to drive under an overpass, the passenger window is shattered, and he is killed.

Jarvis knew that when the president flew in on Air Force One, he always came out in a suit and tie, and the dress code for the visit was suit and tie. And when the president is in the limousine, he is not behind the driver; he is on the right rear side, the position of honor. Still, Jarvis asked Henigman to describe the limo. She correctly said the car was already in Enid. The Secret Service always flies its vehicles to the sites of presidential visits on a cargo plane prior to the visit, storing the vehicles in fire stations or hangars at the airport where Air Force One is to land.

Jarvis asked Henigman to pinpoint just where the limo was. She said it was at the Air Force base near Enid. He asked if she could show him, and she agreed.

As they drove toward the five hangars,

Henigman gave Jarvis directions.

"As we got close to this one hangar, she said to slow down," Jarvis says.

"Something is in that building right there," the woman said.

"What do you mean?" Jarvis asked.

"Something important is in that building there."

"Okay, but not the limo?"

"No," the woman said.

As they drove past another hangar, Henigman said it contained the limo. She then identified another hangar as also containing something important.

Jarvis's hunch was that the limo was in the fire house bordering the runways. As it turned out, he was wrong and the psychic was right. Secret Service agents guard the president's limo until he steps into it. Checking with them, Jarvis learned that the hangar the psychic identified as holding the vehicle did indeed contain two presidential limousines. As the woman walked back to Jarvis's Secret Service car, he asked the special officer in charge of security for the limos what was in the other two hangars she had identified as containing something important.

"He said one contains Marine One, and the other contains other important assets for the president in case of emergencies," Jarvis says.

The woman's claim that Bush would be wearing a sport jacket and would sit behind the driver made Jarvis skeptical, but he immediately briefed supervisors at the Secret Service Intelligence Division duty desk in Washington.

"You guys are going to think I'm crazy," he began, then related the information about the vision and how Henigman had correctly led him to the president's limo.

As Jarvis saw it, "We deal in the bizarre all the time. Nothing's too wacky that hasn't come across the duty desk report sheet. You're just straight up and lay it out the way you see it. And together you examine and turn the thing over and make a determination."

At 1 A.M., Jarvis called the head of the advance team and briefed him. However, since Henigman seemed to be wrong about what clothes Bush would be wearing and where he would be sitting in the limo, they dismissed the psychic's concerns. Still, that morning, before Bush left for Oklahoma, the head of the advance team informed detail leaders based in W-16, where agents are stationed under the Oval Office, about the psychic's vision and the fact that she knew where the presidential limousines were parked.

Jarvis also discussed the matter with the agent in charge of the motorcade. He asked if the motorcade route would take the president by an overpass. The agent said it would go under a railroad overpass and several elevated intersections on Routes 64 and 412 from Enid Woodring Regional Airport.

"Do you have an alternate motorcade route?"

"Sure, we always do," the agent replied.

That morning, Air Force One landed in Enid. Known by the Secret Service code name Angel, Air Force One got its name when Dwight D. Eisenhower — code-named Providence — was president. Because a flight controller mistook the president's plane for a commercial one, the pilot suggested designating any aircraft the president was in as Air Force One.

The current presidential plane is a Boeing 747-200B bubble-top jumbo jet acquired in 1990 when George H. W. Bush was president. It has a range of 9,600 miles and a maximum cruising altitude of 45,100 feet. It cruises at 600 miles per hour but can achieve speeds of 701 miles per hour. The plane is 231 feet long, and its three levels give it 4,000 square feet of floor space. In addition to two pilots, a navigator, and a flight engineer, the plane can carry seventy-six passengers. It is equipped with two galleys, where Air Force One stewards can prepare a hundred meals at one sitting.

Under Federal Aviation Administration regulations, Air Force One takes precedence over all other aircraft. When approaching an airport, it bumps any other planes that have preceded it into the airspace. Before it lands, Secret Service agents on the ground check the runway for explosives or objects such as stray tires. Generally, other aircraft may not land on the same runway for fifteen or twenty minutes before Air Force One lands.

As President Bush came out of Air Force One in Enid, Agent Jarvis stared at him in disbelief. Bush was *not* wearing a suit. He had on an outdoor jacket and an open-collar shirt, just as the psychic had said he would. Bush then walked down the gangway steps and got in on the limousine's right side, his usual position. Jarvis started to relax. But after delivering a short speech in Enid, Bush invited some friends to sit with him in the limo for the four-mile drive back to the airport. They got in first — on the right side. Bush walked around the limo, got in on the left side, and sat down behind the driver. Again, the psychic had been right.

Jarvis and the advance leader decided the psychic could not be ignored. Never mind if anyone thought they were crazy. For the trip back to the airport, the agents ordered the motorcade to take the alternate route along East Market Street and Jerauld Gentry Road. It did not go under an overpass.

No harm befell Bush, and agents never told him what had happened. Nor did anyone check to see if snipers were on any overpasses. In November 1993, a little more than a year after her encounter with the Secret Service, Henigman died at the age of fifty-five.

10
PEANUT FARMER

Jimmy Carter cultivated the image of a jolly populist who grew up on a farm, ran a peanut warehouse, and championed the workingman.

The presidency "is a place of compassion," Carter said in accepting his nomination for a second term at the 1980 Democratic National Convention. "My own heart is burdened for the troubled Americans. The poor and the jobless and the afflicted . . ."

Behind the scenes, it was a different story.

"Carter was just very short and rude most of the time," an agent recalls. "With agents, he'd just pretend like you were not around. You'd say hello, and he'd just look at you, like you weren't there, like you were bothering him."

Carter actually told Secret Service agents and uniformed officers he did not want them to greet him on his way to the Oval Office. It was apparently too much bother for him to have to say hello back to another human being.

Nor did Carter have much use for the military. Even though he was a Naval Academy graduate, Carter "talked down to the military, just talked like they didn't know what they were talking about," a former agent says.

"Carter didn't want military aides to wear uniforms," former agent Cliff Baranowski recalls.

Not surprisingly, of all the presidents in recent memory, Carter was the chief executive most detested by Secret Service agents. Agent John Piasecky was on Carter's detail for three and a half years. That included seven months of driving him in the presidential limousine. Aside from giving directions, Carter never spoke to him, he says.

Carter tried to project an image of himself as man of the people by carrying his own luggage when traveling. But that was another charade. When he was a candidate in 1976, Carter would carry his own bags when the press was around but would ask the Secret Service to carry them the rest of the time.

As president, Carter — code-named Deacon — orchestrated more ruses involving his luggage.

"When he was traveling, he would get on the helicopter and fly to Air Force One at Andrews Air Force Base," says former Secret Service agent Baranowski. "He would roll up his sleeves and carry his bag over his shoulder, but it was empty. He wanted people to think he was carrying his own bag."

"Carter made a big show about taking a hang-up carry-on out of the trunk of the limo when he'd go someplace, and there was nothing in it," says another agent who was on his detail. "It was empty. It was just all show."

Carter would regularly make a show of arriving early at the Oval Office to call attention to how hard he was working for the American people.

"He would walk into the Oval Office at 6 A.M., do a little work for half an hour, then close the curtains and take a nap," says Robert B. Sulliman Jr., who was on Carter's detail. "His staff would tell the press he was working."

Another agent says that at other times, he could see Carter through the Oval Office windows dozing off in his desk chair while he was ostensibly working.

"Carter was a phony, an absolute phony," an agent says.

"When he was in a bad mood, you didn't want to bring him anything," a former Secret Service agent says. "It was this hunkered-down attitude: 'I'm running the show.' It was as if he didn't trust anyone around him. He had that big smile, but when he was in the White House, it was a different story."

"The only time I saw a smile on Carter's face was when the cameras were going," says former agent George Schmalhofer, who was assigned periodically to the Carter detail.

Perhaps because of his aversion to the military, Carter refused to let the military aide with the nuclear football stay in a nearby trailer when Carter was visiting his home in Plains, Georgia.

"Carter did not want the nuclear football at Plains," a former agent says. "There was no place to stay in Plains. The military wanted a trailer there. He didn't want that. So the military aide had to stay in Americus." The town was a fifteen-minute drive from Carter's home. "Carter didn't want anyone bothering him on his property," the former agent explains. "He wanted his privacy."

Terrence Adamson, Carter's lawyer, denied that Carter refused to let the military aide stay near his residence. But Bill Gulley, who was in charge of the operation as director of the White House Military Office, confirmed it.

Carter may have shown no interest in protecting the country from a nuclear attack, but he loved to pore over the inner workings of the White House, including how the air-conditioning worked. He even delved into how the Secret Service transported presidential limousines. Carter decided that to save money, they should be driven across the country instead of flown. Because the Air Force flew the vehicles as part of training, the Secret Service believed that Carter's plan actually increased costs.

A sign of another Carter project, an agent recalls seeing the blueprints for a new submarine on Carter's desk in the private study off the Oval Office.

"I don't know what the hell he was trying to do, figuring out if it would work?" the agent says.

While he publicly denied it, Carter would personally schedule the times when aides could play on the White House tennis courts.

"Carter said, 'I'm in charge,' " a former Secret Service agent says. " 'Everything is my way.' He tried to micromanage everything. You had to go to him about playing on the tennis court. It was ridiculous."

Agents were convinced that Carter as president was in over his head and that Rosalynn was the smarter one. She had a loving relationship with her husband and acted as an advisor, sometimes firmly correcting what he said. Unlike her husband, she treated agents with respect.

"Rosalynn really was the brains of the outfit," says former agent Repasky. "She kept him in line and constantly advised him. She was very pragmatic and organized. He would make an ultra-liberal comment, and she would ground him and tell him he had to be more centrist. If he didn't listen, she could get cold and steely."

"I think the presidency was too big for Carter to comprehend," says former agent Ramon Dunlap.

In recent memory, according to agents, the brattiest offspring of a president was Amy Carter, who was ten when her father became president.

"Amy was spoiled rotten," an agent on her detail says.

"Amy Carter was a mess," says Brad Wells, an Air Force One steward. "She would look at me and pick up a package of [open] soda crackers and crush them and throw them on the floor. She did it purposely. We had to clean it up. That was our job."

Secret Service agents guarding Amy — code-named Dynamo — at school often found themselves in the middle when Amy wanted to play with friends after school instead of going home to the White House to do her homework, as she was supposed to do. When agents told her she had to go home, "Amy would call her father and hand the phone to the agents," Dennis Chomicki, who was on her detail, remembers. "The president would say to take Amy anywhere she wants to go. Amy just had her father wrapped up."

Since Amy would often stay at a friend's house through the evening, agents wound up working longer hours than if they had taken her directly to the White House. As a result, says Chomicki, "the detail would always try to get Mrs. Carter, the first lady, on the phone, because she would say, 'Nothing doing, she's coming home. She's got her homework to do.' "

Of all the presidential children guarded by the Secret Service, Carter's second oldest son, James Earl "Chip" Carter III, was one of the least liked. Twenty-six when his father won the presidency, Chip had helped campaign for him in 1976 and again gave speeches on his behalf when Carter ran for reelection in 1980.

"He was outrageous," a Secret Service agent says. "Chip was out of control. Marijuana, liquor, chasing women." Separated from his wife, Chip would "pick up women in Georgetown and ask if they wanted to have sex in the White House. Most of them did. He did it as often as he could," the agent says.

At one point, Rosalynn Carter told the press that all three of her sons had experimented with marijuana. Their oldest son, John William "Jack" Carter, was discharged by the Navy for smoking weed.

After he left the presidency, Jimmy Carter often went skiing and fishing with Rosalynn in Colorado.

"He'd go skiing, and he'd take lessons, and his wife would take lessons, too," a former agent says. "But he wouldn't listen to his instructor. He thought he was an expert. He'd go skiing, and she'd go skiing, and he'd keep falling down or not doing things right, and she would do everything right the way the instructors taught her. He'd get pissed off because she was a better skier than he was."

The same pattern played out when the couple went fishing.

"She'd go out there in the middle of the stream and go fishing, and he'd be out there thinking he was the best fisherman in the world," the former agent says. "He'd be tossing that line out there, and she'd be catching fish, and he'd get just furious because he couldn't catch a fish and she could."

11
WHITE HOUSE COLLAR

The White House is code-named Crown, and for an assassin, the president is the jewel in the crown. Terrorists, mentally unstable individuals seeking acclaim, lone gunmen with a gripe against the government, and assassins who crave notoriety would all love to take out the president.

Each year, twenty-five to thirty people with mayhem in mind try to ram the White House gates in cars, scale the eight-foot-high reinforced steel fence, shoot their way in, set themselves on fire at the gates, or cause other disruptions. Individuals who demand to see the president confront the Secret Service on a daily basis. Most of the people who cause disruptions around the White House are mentally ill and see the White House as Mecca.

"For the same reason that people stalk the president, the White House is a magnet for the psychotic," former agent Pete Dowling observes. "The president is an authority figure, and many people who have psychoses or have paranoid schizophrenia think that the government is transmitting rays at them or interrupting their thought processes. And what is the ultimate symbol of the government? It's the White House. So many of these people come to the gate at the White House and say they want to have an appointment to see the president or they want to see the president."

Agents and Uniformed Division officers have a name for the arrest of those who cause a disruption at the gates: White House collars.

"Every day there is at least one White House collar," says a former uniformed officer. "Most sane people who really want to harm the president aren't going to actually telegraph it. But you'd have people who would show up and say 'Listen, I demand to talk to the president now. My son's in [the war], and it's his fault. And I'm not leaving until I talk to the president.' At that point, special agents from the Protective Intelligence Squad in the Washington field office come out and interview the guy."

Eventually, agents warn the individual to leave or he will be arrested. In most cases, he complies.

At the White House, "you know right away if there's a fence jumper," a Secret Service agent says. "There are electronic eyes and ground sensors six feet back [from the sidewalk] that are monitored twenty-four hours a day. They sense movement and weight. Infrared detectors are installed closer to the house. You have audio detectors. Every angle is covered by cameras and recorded."

Uniformed Division officers and the division's Emergency Response Team, armed with P90 submachine guns, form the first line of defense.

"If somebody jumps that fence, ERT is going to get them right away, either with a dog or just themselves," an agent says. "They'll give the dog a command, and that dog will knock over a two-hundred-fifty-pound man. It will hit him dead center and take him down." In addition, he says, the Uniformed Division's countersnipers will train their weapons on the intruder.

A suspect who is armed and has jumped the fence may get a warning to drop the weapon. If he does not immediately obey the command, the Secret Service is under orders to take the person out quickly rather than risk a possible hostage-taking situation.

140

Uniformed Division officers protect the White House building complex as well as foreign embassies. Secret Service agents protect individuals: the president and his family, the vice president and his family, former presidents and their spouses, visiting heads of state, and certain White House officials, like the chief of staff and the national security advisor. Agents also protect some Cabinet officers, like the secretary of the treasury and the secretary of homeland security, because they are in the line of succession to the presidency and are not otherwise protected.

As their name implies, Uniformed Division officers wear uniforms, while Secret Service agents wear suits. Unlike Secret Service agents, uniformed officers are required only to have high school diplomas. Nor do they have the background and training of agents. Like agents, they must be U.S. citizens to apply. At the time of their appointment, they must be at least twenty-one years of age but younger than forty. The age limit for special agents is thirty-seven years. Besides passing a background examination, potential agents and uniformed officers must take drug tests and pass a polygraph examination before being hired.

Interestingly, the Secret Service adopted

the term "special agent" for all its agents from the FBI, whose director J. Edgar Hoover had devised it to give G-men more stature.

While most agents say they respect the job uniformed officers do, agents are above them in the pecking order. Agents will refer to Uniformed Division officers as "box creatures," a reference to the fact that they work from box-like guard posts at the White House. Uniformed Division officers, in turn, will refer to agents as "suit guards."

"There is nothing more insulting than calling us guards," says a former uniformed officer who became an agent.

In protecting the White House and providing security at events, the Uniformed Division, which has twelve hundred officers, employs canine units. In all, the agency has seventy-five of the dogs. Mainly Belgian Malinois, most of the dogs are cross-trained to sniff out explosives and attack an intruder. While they resemble German shepherds, the breed is believed to be higher energy and more agile. The dogs are prey-driven, and ball play is their reward after they locate their "prey." The Secret Service pays $4,500 for each trained dog.

While waiting to check cleared vehicles that arrive at the White House's southwest gate, the dogs stand on a white concrete pad that is refrigerated in summer so their paws don't get hot. Each dog eagerly checks out about a hundred cars a day.

For new recruits, there's a seventeen-week canine school at the Secret Service training facility, where dogs are paired with handlers. The dogs come to the school with a lot of training behind them, but the Secret Service gives them more — in explosive detection and emergency response to threats such as a fence jumper at the White House.

The Secret Service's Technical Security Division (TSD) installs sensors to pinpoint intruders on the White House grounds and devices that detect radiation and explosives at entrances to the White House. TSD also samples the air and water within the White House for contaminants, radioactivity, and deadly bacteria. As a precaution, air in the White House is maintained at high pressure to expel possible contaminants.

Populated with real-life Qs, James Bond's fictional gadget master, TSD sweeps the White House and hotel rooms for electronic bugs. While electronic bugs have never been found in the White House, sweeps of hotel rooms have detected bugs that had been planted to pick up the conversations of previous guests. When suspicious packages are thrown onto the White House grounds, TSD deploys robots to examine them safely.

At an off-site location, TSD each year screens more than a million pieces of mail addressed to the White House for pathogens and other biological threats before it is delivered. With Los Alamos National Laboratory or Sandia National Laboratories, TSD runs top secret risk assessments to find any holes in physical or cyber security measures.

In case an assassin bent on hunting down the president manages to penetrate all the security, TSD installs panic buttons and alarms in the Oval Office and the residence part of the White House. The alarms can be activated in case of a physical threat or a medical emergency. Many of the alarm triggers are small presidential seals placed innocuously on tables or desks. Knocking them over activates them and brings agents running, weapons drawn.

In addition, "There are knock-down alarms that may be lamps," a current agent says. "The president or vice president knocks a lamp down if he needs help."

Besides agents and uniformed officers stationed around the Oval Office, in response to an alarm, agents deployed to W-16, the Secret Service holding room under the Oval Office, can leap up the stairway in a few seconds with their weapons drawn.

As a last resort, the White House has emergency escape routes, including a tunnel ten feet wide and seven feet high. It extends from a subbasement under the east wing of the White House to the basement of the Treasury Department, adjacent to the White House grounds. A new multistory underground bunker can accommodate the entire White House staff so the West Wing can continue to operate in the event of an attack.

Incidents at the White House always seem to have a bizarre quality. At 9:04 P.M. on Friday, November 11, 2011, U.S. Park Police responded to reports of gunshots along Constitution Avenue, at Seventeenth Street near the Ellipse and the Washington Monument, about a half mile south of the White House. A witness said she saw the driver of a dark-colored sedan firing a weapon through the passenger window in the direction of the White House.

Officers searching the area spotted a black 1998 Honda Accord parked on the lawn of the United States Institute of Peace, near the ramp from Constitution Avenue to the Theodore Roosevelt Bridge. A witness said he saw the driver try unsuccessfully to restart the car, then run. Inside the car was a Romanian-made Cugir SA semiautomatic rifle with a large scope.

According to a Secret Service agent, while a Uniformed Division officer at the White House reported over his radio on Friday night that shots were being fired at the White House, "a Uniformed Division supervisor got on the radio and said to disregard that, there weren't shots fired, it was construction in the area." The agent notes that while there was construction in the area, "it had stopped for the night, and what that officer initially said was right on."

No action was taken until five days later. That was when the FBI, pursuing the shooting, found a bullet hole in a window on the south side of the White House, confirming the uniformed officer's report on Friday night. The slug had pierced the historic exterior glass, but ballistic glass installed behind that glass stopped the round. The FBI found several other bullet impact points on the south side of the building on or above the second floor.

At least one of the bullets recovered at the White House matched the ammunition and nine spent cartridges found in the Honda, according to an affidavit an FBI agent filed the next day with the U.S. District Court in Washington. It supported an arrest warrant for Oscar Ramiro Ortega-Hernandez, the owner of the abandoned Honda.

A month earlier, before leaving his home in Idaho Falls, Idaho, Ortega-Hernandez had told acquaintances that Obama was "the devil" and "the Antichrist" and said that he "needed to kill him." The twenty-one-year-old made a video asking Oprah Winfrey to let him appear on television with her.

"You see, Oprah, there is still so much more that God needs me to express to the world," he says in the video. "It's not just a coincidence that I look like Jesus. I am the modern-day Jesus Christ that you all have been waiting for."

On November 16, Pennsylvania state police arrested Ortega-Hernandez at a motel in Indiana, Pennsylvania. He was charged with attempting to assassinate the president and pleaded not guilty. As it happened, both Obamas were out of town when the shooting occurred. The Secret Service never explained to the public why it had taken the agency five days to recognize that the White House had been shot at.

A far more embarrassing incident took place on February 17, 1974, when U.S.

Army private first class Robert K. Preston stole an Army helicopter from Fort Meade, Maryland, and landed on the South Lawn at 9:30 P.M.

Instead of firing at the helicopter, uniformed officers called a Secret Service official at home and asked what they should do. He told them to shoot at the helicopter. By then, the helicopter had flown away, but it returned fifty minutes later. This time, uniformed officers and Secret Service agents fired at it with shotguns and submachine guns.

"They riddled it with bullets," a Secret Service agent says. "When he landed [the second time], he opened the door and rolled under the helicopter. It probably saved his life. They put seventy rounds through that. There were twenty rounds in the seat. He would have been shot to death [if he had not rolled under the chopper]. It was not going to take off this time."

Preston, age twenty, had flunked out of flight school and perhaps wanted to prove that he did have some flying skills. He was treated for a superficial gunshot wound, sentenced to a year at hard labor, and fined $2,400. Neither President Nixon nor his wife, Pat, was at the White House at the time.

One of the more dramatic attacks took place on October 29, 1994, at 2:55 P.M., when Francisco Martin Duran stood on the south sidewalk of Pennsylvania Avenue and began firing at the White House with a Chinese SKS semiautomatic rifle. As he ran toward Fifteenth Street, he paused to reload, and a tourist tackled him. Uniformed officers drew their weapons, but they held fire as more tourists grappled with Duran.

"I wish you had shot me," Duran told officers as they arrested him.

When Duran began firing, a white-haired man who resembled President Clinton had just come out of the White House. The Secret Service concluded that Duran likely thought he was firing at Clinton. Duran was convicted of attempting to assassinate the president and sentenced to forty years in prison. He was also ordered to pay the government $3,200 to repair damage to the White House, including replacing windows in the press room that were riddled with bullets.

A previous incident, on September 11, 1994, demonstrated the White House's vulnerability. That evening, after drinking heavily and smoking crack cocaine, Frank E. Corder found the keys to a Cessna P150 rental airplane at the Harford County

Airport in Churchville, Maryland. Although the thirty-eight-year-old truck driver was not a licensed pilot, he had taken some lessons and several times had flown that particular aircraft.

Corder stole the plane and flew to the White House. He then dove the plane directly toward it at a steep angle. While aircraft are not supposed to fly over the White House, airplanes periodically do so by mistake. As a result, the military must exercise judgment when deciding whether to shoot down aircraft that stray into White House airspace.

Given that after 9/11 cockpits of commercial airliners were hardened, air marshals were assigned to flights, and many pilots are now armed, it is less likely that a commercial airliner would again be successfully commandeered. But since 9/11, any general aviation aircraft that violates restrictions on flights near the White House and does not respond to military commands is to be shot down by missiles or fighter aircraft.

The Joint Operations Center at Secret Service headquarters now interfaces twenty-four hours a day with the Federal Aviation Administration and the control tower at Washington's Reagan National Airport.

Headquarters also views on radar any planes flying in the area.

Corder's plane crashed onto the White House lawn just south of the Executive Mansion at 1:49 A.M. and skidded across the ground. But Corder had not planned on the Sony JumboTron that had been set up for an event next to the White House on the South Lawn. The giant television screen measured 33 feet by 110 feet.

"There's no way he could have flown the plane into the White House," says Pete Dowling, who was on the President's Protective Detail at the time. "He couldn't have navigated the plane without hitting the JumboTron. So he had to land a little bit early, and what he did was he just came to rest against one of the magnolias that was right in front of the south part of the White House."

Corder died of multiple massive blunt-force injuries from the crash. At the time, the White House was undergoing renovations, and President Clinton and his family were staying at Blair House, the guest house for presidents and dignitaries on Pennsylvania Avenue across the street from the Eisenhower Executive Office Building and next to the White House.

While Corder had expressed dissatisfaction with Clinton's policies, and his third marriage had just crumbled, the Secret Service concluded that his purpose was to gain notoriety. He had told friends he wanted to "kill himself in a big way" by flying into the White House or the Capitol.

Indeed, for many White House collars, causing mayhem at the Capitol is a backup plan if security at the White House proves too tight. Thus, Miriam Carey, a thirty-four-year-old dental hygienist from Stamford, Connecticut, first tried to drive her black Infiniti through a White House checkpoint at Fifteenth and E Streets NW at 2:12 P.M. on October 3, 2013.

"Whoa! Whoa!" Secret Service uniformed officers shouted as an officer tried to stop her car with a bike rack barricade. Her car hit the officer, who was thrown up on the hood and then off the car. She made a U-turn and led uniformed officers on a chase that reached speeds of eighty miles per hour along Pennsylvania Avenue toward the Capitol, where officers ordered occupants to "shelter in place."

As officers shot at Carey and tried to corner her at Garfield Circle, she rammed a Secret Service vehicle. She then backed up the car and drove to Constitution Avenue and Second Street NE, where a barricade operated by the Capitol Police popped up from the street and stopped her. She attempted to make another U-turn, but the car became stuck on a grassy divide. At 2:20 P.M., outside the Hart Senate Office Building, Carey was shot and killed. Officers rescued her one-year-old daughter, who was in the car with her.

Like most White House collars, Carey was suffering from mental illness. She had postpartum psychosis and schizophrenia. She was convinced Obama had placed her home town of Stamford on lockdown and that he was communicating to her electronically.

12
BOYS WILL BE BOYS

Unlike Jimmy Carter, Secret Service agents found that Ronald Reagan was the same decent, affable man in private that he appeared to be in public.

"What you saw with President Reagan in private with us at Camp David, at the ranch in Santa Barbara, was exactly the same way he came across on TV," says Patrick Sullivan, an agent on Reagan's detail for the last four years of his presidency. "He was just a very nice guy who was concerned about us and our creature comforts."

So that agents and the staff would be home with their families on Christmas Day, President Reagan would stay at the White House for Christmas, Sullivan says. Then on December 26, "he would head out to the Century Plaza Hotel in Los Angeles, and we'd stay there for a couple of days."

When the Reagans made an exception one year and stayed at the ranch on Christmas

Day, Reagan "came up to me and apologized to me for having to be away from my family on a holiday," former agent Cliff Baranowski recalls. "A lot of times they would give us food from a party. I certainly did not expect it, but sometimes they insisted."

"When he [Reagan] first became president, he called down to the Los Angeles field office from his home there and he said, 'I want every one of your agents up here because I want to get a picture with all of them,' " former agent Lloyd Bulman says. "And he had all the agents come up there and take their pictures with him, and he signed an autographed picture for them."

"The military and the police loved him," Sullivan says. "When he returned to Air Force One, he would never fail to have all the police officers from his motorcade line up at the stairs of Air Force One so that he would get a handshake individually with each one of them, and they'd take a picture and then they would get those pictures out to them."

Reagan liked to walk around the West Wing and Eisenhower Executive Office Building and surprise employees.

"On one occasion, an elderly lady was typing away at some document," former agent

Dennis Chomicki recalls. "The president walked in, and she was so busy working she didn't even notice him. The president picked up the document and he says, 'Can I look at this?' She grabbed it out of his hand and she goes, 'That's classified!' Then she looked up and saw it was the president, and she goes, 'Oh my God, you can look at it!' "

Whenever Reagan boarded Air Force One or Marine One, he made a point of greeting the pilot and copilot.

"Carter came into the cockpit once in the two years I was on with him," says James A. Buzzelli, an Air Force One flight engineer. "But [Ronald] Reagan never got on or off without sticking his head in the cockpit and saying, 'Thanks, fellas,' or 'Have a nice day.' He was just as personable in person as he came across to the public."

When Reagan was running for president the first time, he came out of his home in Bel Air to drive to his ranch. An agent noticed that he was wearing a pistol and asked what that was for.

"Well, just in case you guys can't do the job, I can help out," Reagan — code-named Rawhide — replied, according to former agent Thomas Blecha. Reagan confided to one agent that on his first presidential trip to the Soviet Union in May 1988, he had

156

carried a gun in his briefcase.

Reagan had a routine at Rancho del Cielo, his seven-hundred-acre ranch north of Santa Barbara.

"Reagan would get up, and he and Nancy would sit around for a while," Sullivan says. "Then they'd go ride horses and come back and have lunch. And then he would wait until we'd change shifts at 2:30 P.M. before he'd go out and cut wood, because he knew that if he went out in the woods with the day shift guys, they'd be stuck out there for a couple of extra hours."

Reagan quietly wrote personal checks to people who had written him with hard luck stories.

"Reagan was famous for firing up Air Force jets on behalf of children who needed transport for kidney operations," says Frank J. Kelly, who drafted presidential messages. "These are things you never knew about. He never bragged about it. I hand-carried checks for four thousand or five thousand dollars to people who had written him. He would say, 'Don't tell people. I was poor myself.'"

While Reagan liked to look for the best in people, he was not a choirboy. On one occasion, he gave a speech at Georgetown University, and as the motorcade drove

157

down M Street to return to the White House, Reagan noticed a man in a crowd.

"Fellows, look," he said to his agents. "A guy over there's giving me the finger, can you believe that?"

Reagan started waving back, smiling.

"We're going by, and he's still waving and smiling, and he goes, 'Hi there, you son of a bitch,'" former agent Chomicki remembers. Like many agents, Chomicki does dead-on impressions. He imitates Reagan's buttery smooth delivery.

When the news broke that Democratic presidential candidate Gary Hart was having an affair with Donna Rice, Reagan was returning to the White House from an evening event.

"We were in the elevator going up to the residence on the second floor of the White House," says former agent Ted Hresko. "The door of the elevator was about to close, and one of the staffers blocked it. The staffer told Reagan the news about Donna Rice and Gary Hart."

Reagan nodded his head and looked at Agent Hresko.

"Boys will be boys," he said to the agent.

When the door of the elevator shut, Reagan added firmly, "But boys will not be president."

Until the *Miami Herald* revealed Hart's fling with Rice in May 1987, the media had not exposed extramarital affairs of presidents and presidential candidates. Yet the hypocrisy and lack of judgment exhibited by a politician engaging in such relations are arguably clues to character that the electorate should consider.

In fact, there was more to the Hart story. According to a former Secret Service agent who was on the candidate's detail, well before his encounter with Rice, Senator Hart routinely cavorted with stunning models and actresses in Los Angeles, courtesy of one of his political advisors, actor Warren Beatty.

"Warren Beatty gave him a key to his house on Mulholland Drive," the agent says. "It was near Jack Nicholson's house." Beatty would arrange to have twenty-year-old women — "tens," as the agent described them — meet Senator Hart at Beatty's house.

"Hart would say, 'We're expecting a guest,'" the former agent says. "When it was warm, they would wear bikinis and jump in the hot tub in the back. Once in the tub, their tops would often come off. Then they would go into the house. The guests stayed well into the night and often left just before sunrise. Beatty was a bachelor, but Hart was a senator running for president and was married."

"Sometimes," the agent says, "there were two or three girls with him at a time. We would say, 'There goes a ten. There's a nine. Did you see that? Can you believe that?' Hart did not care. He was like a kid in a candy store."

Asked for comment, Gayle Samek, his spokesperson, said, "Senator Hart tends to focus on the present rather than the past, so there's no comment."

When John Hinckley shot Reagan at the Washington Hilton, the military aide with the nuclear football took off for the White House, where agents were taking the president. But that plan soon changed.

"I checked him over and found no blood," Agent Jerry Parr says. "After fifteen or twenty seconds, we were under Dupont Circle moving fast. President Reagan had a napkin from the speech and dabbed his mouth with it. He said, 'I think I cut the inside of my mouth.' "

Parr noticed that the blood was bright red and frothy. Recognizing that as a danger sign, he ordered the driver to head toward George Washington Hospital Center. It was the hospital that had been preselected in the event medical assistance was needed.

It turned out that the president may have been within minutes of death when he arrived at the hospital. Going straight there probably saved his life. Reagan not only was separated from the football during that time, but the FBI confiscated all his clothing and personal effects at the hospital as evidence. That included the card with codes for authenticating the president's identity so he could launch a nuclear strike.

"We sat in the office the next day and looked at this thing, and then we found out [what the card was]," Thomas J. Baker, who was in charge of the FBI response at the Washington field office, tells me. "It looked basically like a credit card or an ATM card," says Baker, who was the assistant special agent in charge of criminal investigations and the first FBI agent on the scene at the shooting. "It had some holes punched through it."

Despite a demand by James V. Hickey Jr., then the director of the White House Military Office, the FBI held on to the authenticator card for two weeks. Under the Twenty-fifth Amendment to the Constitution, the president may transmit to the president pro tempore of the Senate and the speaker of the House of Representatives a written declaration that he is unable to discharge the powers and duties of his office, transferring power automatically to the vice president as acting president. That is what Reagan did before undergoing surgery. But just prior to that, as agents carried him to trauma bay five in the emergency room, he was unconscious.

Incredibly, at the time, no procedure was in place to delegate authority immediately when a president is disabled. Under the Twenty-fifth Amendment, the vice president and a majority of the Cabinet would have to transmit to the president pro tempore of the Senate and the speaker of the House a declaration that the president was unable to discharge his duties. But until that took place, it was not clear who could launch a nuclear strike while Reagan was incapacitated. As vice president, George H. W. Bush could have taken it upon himself to authorize a strike by calling the defense secretary through secure communications provided by the nuclear football, but even the vice president may not have had legal authority to do so.

When Bush became president, his administration drafted a highly detailed, classified plan for immediate transfer of power in case a president is unable to discharge his duties. In that event, the vice president or the next official in the line of succession is informed by the senior staff member with the president or the national security advisor, or, if they have been taken out, the Defense Department duty officer, and that individual automatically becomes acting president, according to John Stufflebeem, who oversaw the Defense Department program that deploys the nuclear football.

"If you cannot execute duties as commander in chief, you are ipso facto not the president," Stufflebeem says. "That authority is transferred to somebody who can execute that authority to be commander in chief."

Even after having been shot, Reagan displayed his sense of humor. To his doctors, he said, "I just hope you're Republicans." To which one doctor replied, "Today, Mr. President, we're all Republicans."

Reagan shared his sense of humor with his agents.

"He'd hear a joke from one of his buddies, and the next thing you know, he'd be telling us as we're walking somewhere," former agent Sullivan says. "If it was a little off-color, he'd make sure no female agents were around because he was just a real gentleman."

After Reagan left office, he was to speak at an event in Akron, Ohio. In contrast to the retinue he had had as president, Reagan traveled with just one staffer and his Secret Service contingent. The agent in charge of the former president's protective detail poked his head into the command post. He said to Agent Pete Dowling, "You know, the president's been sitting in his room alone all morning. And he'd really like for some folks to talk to. Would you guys mind if he came over and sat in the command post and just chatted with you guys for a while?"

"That'd be terrific, bring him over," Dowling said.

For two hours, Reagan chatted with the agents, telling stories and jokes.

"He told us he and Mikhail Gorbachev had private conversations," Dowling says. "They agreed that their talks were not about today and are not about us. They're about our grandchildren and the life that they're going to live."

While in office, Reagan never showed the effects of Alzheimer's disease, which ulti- mately led to his death. "We had a hundred twenty agents on his detail, and he seemed to remember everyone's name," former agent Glenn Smith says.

But in March 1993, a year before he announced that he was suffering from Alzheimer's, Reagan honored Canadian prime minister Brian Mulroney at his library and invited him to his ranch. As Mulroney was leaving, the prime minister asked Agent Chomicki, "Do you notice something with the president?"

Chomicki said he did but did not know what the problem was.

"He would just stop in mid-sentence and forget what he was saying," Chomicki recalls. "Then he would just start a whole new story." While Reagan was in office, "I never noticed anything like that."

After he was diagnosed with Alzheimer's, Reagan remarked, "Well, there must be a positive side to this. Maybe I'll get to meet new people every day," former agent Sullivan says. "He tried to make light of it, which is classic Ronald Reagan," Sullivan observes. "Even though there was bad news, he'd try to put you at ease."

As the disease progressed, Reagan stopped going to his office and playing golf.

"Reagan would watch TV, and we would take him on walks," Fred Fukunaga, an agent who was with him almost to the end, says. "He was still innately kind and loved seeing little kids. He was always joking around."

13
A BULLET FOR THE PRESIDENT

The Secret Service's training facility is spread over 440 acres between a wildlife refuge and a soil conservation area in Laurel, Maryland. The forest muffles the gunfire, the squealing wheels, and the explosions that are the sounds of training Secret Service agents and Secret Service Uniformed Division officers.

Here at the James J. Rowley Training Center, agent trainees receive sixteen weeks of training. In addition, they receive twelve and a half weeks of training at the Federal Law Enforcement Training Center (FLETC) in Glynco, Georgia.

Each year, the training center graduates seven to eleven classes of twenty-four Secret Service and Uniformed Division recruits. Even though the training center is in Laurel, agents refer to it as "Beltsville," which is actually the town next door. Most of the training center's roads have names appropriate to the task at hand: Firearms Road, Range Road, Action Road, and Perimeter Road. Nothing called Ambush Road, but there is always an ambush in the works.

At what the Secret Service calls Hogan's Alley — not to be confused with the FBI's Hogan's Alley at its Quantico, Virginia, training academy — instructors set up scenarios to show trainees how to take down the bad guys. Except for a real two-story house and soft drink machine, the block-long village is like a Hollywood set. It has façades of a hardware store, a hotel, a restaurant, a bar, and a bank. Real cars are parked in front.

Narrating one of the scenarios, Bobbie McDonald, assistant to the special agent in charge of training, explains, "What we're viewing is how they come upon the problem, how they alert about the problem, how they alert their partner, how they react to the situation. Did they take cover? Did they draw their weapon in an appropriate fashion and at an appropriate time? Did they shoot when they should have? Was it what we would call a good shoot, versus a bad shoot?"

Down the road, a smoke bomb goes off near a motorcade. The counterassault team jumps out to deal with whatever it encounters — a motorcade ambush, a suicide bomber, a shooter. Perhaps the explosion is a distraction from the real threat. The team leader sees something in the woods, a sniper hiding behind a tree. "Sniper subdued," the instructor says. "The problem" has been dealt with. The team jumps back into the van. The motorcade reassembles and drives off to continue around campus, where more dangers await. These could be a series of "instant action drills," where motorcades are attacked, snipers fire from windows, and anything may blow up.

Trainees learn to respond to threats and take turns playing the protectee. They rehearse responding to an assailant by using pressure points to unlock his grip. When trainees interview a "subject" in the lockup room, the person is usually a contracted role player — an actor or a retired police officer.

At the protective operations driving course, trainees receive about twenty-four hours of training in driving techniques. Agents who are about to be assigned to drive in a motorcade receive an additional forty hours of training.

Driver training is carried out on a giant parking lot that looks like the obstacle course from a TV commercial or a reality show. Here they use Chargers — high-powered, high-energy vehicles — to speed out of the kill zone. As a counter-measure, drivers learn to execute the J-turn, making a perfect 180-degree turn at high speed by shifting into reverse, jerking the wheel to the right or left, and shifting into drive.

Trainees learn to negotiate serpentine courses, weaving around objects in the road and crashing through barriers, roadblocks, and other cars. In case a protectee's car is disabled, they learn to push it through turns and obstacles using another vehicle. When backing up, agents are trained not to turn around to look out the rear window. Instead, they must learn to use their side-view mirrors so they can maneuver more rapidly.

At several indoor and outdoor firing ranges, trainees and Secret Service agents practice shooting handguns, shotguns, and automatic weapons.

Everyone has heard that a Secret Service agent could take a bullet for the president. But the idea behind their training is to prevent that from ever happening.

"People always say to me, 'Hey, would you really take a bullet for the president?' " says former agent Pete Dowling. "I say, 'What do you think, I'm stupid?' But what we'll do is we'll do everything in our power to keep the bullet out of the event. And that's what the Secret Service is all about. It's about being prepared, it's about meticulous advance preparation, and it's about training properly, so that when you do your job, you don't have to bumble around for the steps that you take."

"What we are trained to do as shift agents is to cover and evacuate if there is an attack," an agent explains. "We form a human shield around the protectee and get him out of the danger area, to a safer location. If an agent is shot during the evacuation, then that is something that is expected. We rely on our layers of security to handle the attacker, while the inside shift's main function is to get the heck out of Dodge."

As McDonald puts it, "Everything we teach out here, we hope we never have to do."

A key part of the training focuses on previous assassinations and assassination attempts and what can be learned from them. Six years after John Hinckley shot President Reagan, the Secret Service's Office of Training assigned agent William Albracht to teach what was called the "Reagan Attempt." Along with a range of other topics, including actual assassinations, Albracht taught the course as a senior instructor for two years.

In preparing for the sensitive assignment, Albracht read all the Secret Service interviews with the agents who were involved in the incident, studied Hinckley's history, examined the shooting site, watched video and reviewed photos taken that day, and interviewed the agents who were with Reagan and did the advance. He then taught the class to agents who had actually witnessed the incident to make sure everything was accurate in the course he would teach to new agents.

Even though his findings would have been the lead story in newspapers throughout the country if they had ever become public, Secret Service management under Director John R. Simpson approved them and certified Albracht to teach the course at the Rowley Training Center.

On the one hand, Albracht taught that the agents performed magnificently.

"Hinckley discharged his Rohm .22 cal. RG-14 pistol six times," according to his class synopsis. "Reagan press secretary James Brady was hit in the head with the first shot as he walked to the motorcade."

The second shot hit Metropolitan Police officer Thomas Delahanty in the left shoulder and traveled to his spine area, the synopsis says.

"Agent Tim McCarthy, who was assigned to the President's Protective Detail, was hit by Hinckley's third shot as he turned to respond to the threat and assumed a blocking position, spreading his arms in front of Reagan as Reagan was being pushed into the limousine. McCarthy took a bullet from Hinckley in the stomach," according to the synopsis.

The fourth shot hit the right rear window of the president's limo. The fifth shot hit the right rear limo panel. It flattened out like a dime, ricocheted, and traveled through the space between the limo body and the now opened right rear door. That was the round that penetrated Reagan under his seventh rib on the left side. The round then tumbled through his left lung and stopped two inches from his heart.

Hinckley's sixth and final shot went wide of its mark and hit no one.

"This was due to the quick response of Agent D. V. McCarthy," the synopsis says. "When Hinckley opened fire, McCarthy leapt across the crowd and grabbed Hinckley as he pulled the trigger for the last time. He grabbed Hinckley's gun and diverted his aim. McCarthy's instinctive reaction is the reason there was not yet another casualty. To fully comprehend how incredibly quick his response was, it should be noted that Hinckley fired all six shots in 1.48 seconds."

Equally impressive, three seconds after the first shot was fired, Special Agent in Charge Jerry Parr pushed President Reagan into the armored limo.

"Ten seconds after the first shot, the presidential limo departed the area, initially en route to the White House complex," the synopsis notes. "But after SAIC Parr realized that Reagan had been wounded, he diverted to George Washington Hospital ER. This decision alone is credited with saving the life of POTUS."

That day, the agents acted with "utter disregard for their own personal safety," Albracht concluded. "They placed themselves directly in harm's way with little to no thought to anything other than their duty."

But heroic though the agents were, Albracht determined that the reason Hinckley was able to get a shot at Reagan was that the Reagan White House had ordered agents to allow unscreened members of the public to get close to the president to greet him as he left the Washington Hilton.

As part of a cover-up of what really happened, an internal Secret Service inspection report posed this question: "Why was the accused gunman allowed to get so close to the president, and if it was a designated press area, how was he able to penetrate it? Even if it was a designated press area, why was it located so close to the presidential motorcade?"

In answer, the March 31, 1981, inspection report said, "The area was not a designated press area, but rather was open to the general public. We would prefer to keep these public areas further away, but this area was positioned within accepted standards."

Continuing the cover-up, the inspection report posed a second question: "Why wasn't a security perimeter established further from the president's path and the people within the area more closely scrutinized?" In answer, the inspection report said, "The people within the area were under surveillance. The distance is a matter of judgment and civil rights as to how much an area can be restricted."

But the training center synopsis sets forth the damning facts. It says the Reagan White House staff overruled the Secret Service and demanded that the public be allowed without any magnetometer screening within about fifteen feet of the president as he left the hotel.

"John Hinckley, a mentally deranged individual, prepositioned himself in a general public area that the White House staff had requested," the course synopsis says flatly. "To the White House staff, this was an issue of letting the people see their president. They did not feel that the potential risk factor outweighed the positive PR."

In fact, contrary to the inspection report's claim that the public's access to the president was "within accepted standards," the Secret Service's Washington field office advance agent and the Presidential Protection Division advance agent both objected to letting the public into the area, Albracht states.

"They looked on it as an unneeded security risk," the synopsis says. "They wanted zero press or public in the area that would be considered within handgun range. The countersniper teams and the advance security checks on nearby buildings would have taken care of snipers at a greater distance from the hotel entrance."

When the Secret Service and the White House staff disagree on security arrangements, "the USSS advance attempts to work out the issue," the synopsis says. "If an acceptable solution cannot be agreed upon, the matter is kicked upstairs to the USSS detail supervisors and the White House advance office."

However, "in these matters, the White House staff usually trumps the USSS unless a direct link can be shown to a potential threat," the synopsis continues. "In the case of the public area in proximity to Reagan's arrival and departure, based on the intelligence on hand, a direct link could not be made — only that it was a security concern, and we wanted a sterile environment. As a result, the general public area where Hinckley stood fifteen feet, seven inches from the leader of the free world was open to all."

In other words, unless the Secret Service had a crystal ball and knew in advance that Hinckley was planning to shoot the president that day as Reagan left the hotel, agents would have to bow to the wishes of the White House and let the unscreened public get close to the president.

In its effort to whitewash what had happened, the Secret Service tried to shift blame to the FBI, telling Congress that the bureau never told the Secret Service that on October 9, 1980, Nashville International Airport security officers had arrested Hinckley on a charge of illegal possession of three pistols. The Secret Service tried to claim that the arrest had something to do with President Carter's arrival in Nashville that day and therefore the FBI should have conveyed a warning that Hinckley was stalking presidents. Hinckley's pistols were uncovered when his suitcase was screened as he was about to take off for New York. But while the FBI knew about the arrest, nothing tied Hinckley — or any one of thousands of others arrested by the Nashville police around that time — to the president.

"We had nothing to connect Hinckley with stalking Mr. Carter," Darrell Long, an airport security officer who made the arrest, later said.

Even if a connection had been made to the president's visit, the Secret Service could not have prevented Hinckley from traveling six months later to Washington, where he read in the *Washington Post* that Reagan would be speaking that day at the Washington Hilton.

H. Stuart Knight, who was Secret Service director when the shooting occurred, never revealed what really happened. Indeed, Knight and other Secret Service officials who testified to Congress claimed, looking back, that they saw no reason to change the Secret Service's protective procedures.

However, Knight was happy to point fingers at the FBI. Asked in a Senate hearing what the Secret Service might have done if it had known about Hinckley's previous arrest and had connected it with Carter's arrival in Nashville, Knight said lamely, "At a minimum, we would have interviewed the gentleman, and perhaps something more, I don't know."

Similarly, an August 1981 report on the incident by the Treasury Department, which then included the Secret Service before it was moved to the Department of Homeland Security, concealed the real story. Prepared by the Treasury Department's general counsel Peter J. Wallison, it referred vaguely to a need for the Secret Service to work more closely with the White House in setting up protection procedures.

As the Treasury report was about to come out, Wallison frankly told the Associated Press that he would leave questions of who should be allowed near the president and how close they should be to the "political people and to the people with more expertise in protection." In other words, by Wallison's own account, the investigation into why the tragedy happened would not address that question.

In commenting for this book, Wallison,

who later served as Reagan's White House counsel during the president's second term, confirmed that he learned from his interviews with Secret Service agents who were involved that the agents wanted Reagan to be in a secure environment as he left the Washington Hilton, but the Reagan White House staff overruled them.

"The staff had wanted the president to be seen by the media and the public as he came out from the speech," Wallison said, while the Secret Service "fought that." He added, "My view now would be that as soon as there is a problem and the president was shot at and hit, the people in the White House were wrong."

After the shooting, the White House gladly acceded to Secret Service wishes.

"Things such as magnetometers and sterile arrival and departure areas became standard operating procedure," Albracht's class synopsis says. An August 19, 1981, Associated Press story on the Treasury Department report confirmed that security around the president had become "noticeably tighter" since the shooting, with "reporters and others being kept at greater distances."

Based on his own experience as an agent, Albracht notes that those tight procedures continued and in fact became more stringent into the early years of George W. Bush's presidency, when Albracht retired. But as documented in this book, after the Department of Homeland Security took over the Secret Service in 2003, corner cutting — such as allowing people into events without magnetometer screening — again became prevalent.

LEFT: Vice President Joe Biden regularly orders the Secret Service to keep his military aide with the nuclear football a mile behind his motorcade, potentially leaving the country unable to retaliate in the event of a nuclear attack.
Associated Press

BELOW: Secret Service agents discovered that former president Bill Clinton has a blond, well-endowed mistress who lives near the Clintons' home in Chappaqua, New York. As soon as Hillary Clinton leaves, the mistress shows up.
Associated Press

Because Hillary Clinton is so nasty to agents, being assigned to her protective detail is considered a form of punishment and the worst assignment in the Secret Service. *Associated Press*

The Secret Service covered up the fact that President Ronald Reagan's White House staff overruled the Secret Service to let unscreened spectators get close to Reagan as he left the Washington Hilton, allowing John W. Hinckley Jr. to shoot the president. *Associated Press*

Vice President Joe Biden has racked up costs to taxpayers of a million dollars to fly to and from his home in Delaware on Air Force Two. His office tried to cover up the costs of the personal trips. *Associated Press*

Secret Service agents were ordered to ignore security rules and allow the SUV carrying actor Bradley Cooper to drive unscreened into a secure, restricted area when President Obama was about to give his speech at the White House Correspondents Dinner. *Corbis*

Secret Service director Mark Sullivan diverted agents from their protective duties, including watching for snipers as President Obama and his family lifted off in Marine One, and ordered them instead to protect his assistant at her home as a favor to her. *Corbis*

While under Secret Service protection, Jenna Bush bamboozled agents and purposely lost her detail. *Associated Press*

Richard Nixon's close friends Charles "Bebe" Rebozo (right) and Robert Abplanalp tried to smuggle a nude stripper into Nixon's home at the Florida White House in Key Biscayne when the president was there, according to Secret Service agents. *Associated Press*

After leaving the presidency and being afflicted with Alzheimer's disease, Ronald Reagan could no longer go riding with his wife, Nancy, at their California ranch. "Well, there must be a positive side to this," the former president remarked to a Secret Service agent. "Maybe I'll get to meet new people every day." *Associated Press*

Under pressure from White House or campaign staffs, the Secret Service regularly lets people into events without magnetometer screening. *U.S. Secret Service*

Secret Service management's failure to back agents and a culture that condones cutting corners led uniformed officers to allow party crashers Tareq and Michaele Salahi and Carlos Allen into a state dinner at the White House. *Associated Press*

Because the Secret Service would not provide enough magnetometers at his campaign events, Mitt Romney regularly left himself open to assassination by giving speeches to outside crowds that had not been screened. *Associated Press*

At the James J. Rowley Training Center, the Secret Service gives new agents firearms training and wows members of Congress with supposedly spontaneous scenarios that are actually secretly rehearsed beforehand. *U.S. Secret Service*

The Secret Service keeps the presidential limousine, known as the Beast, in the garage under its headquarters. *Pamela Kessler*

Secret Service dogs are cross-trained to sniff out explosives and attack an intruder. The dogs are prey-driven, and ball play—shown here in the basement of Secret Service headquarters—is their reward after they locate their "prey." *Pamela Kessler*

The Secret Service's Technical Security Division installs sensors to pinpoint intruders on the White House grounds and deploys devices that detect radiation and explosives at entrances to the White House. *White House*

14
NANCY

Unlike her husband, Nancy Reagan —
code-named Rainbow — could be aloof and
demanding.

Nancy was "very cold," a Secret Service
agent assigned to her detail says. "She had
her circle of four friends in Los Angeles,
and that was it. Nothing changed when she
was with her kids. She made it clear to her
kids that if they wanted to see their father,
they had to check with her first. It was a
standing rule. Not that they could not see
him. 'I will let you know if it is advisable
and when you can see him.' She was something else."

If Nancy Reagan's wealthy California
friends reported getting their copies of
Vogue and *Mademoiselle* before she did, she
took it out on the White House staff. For
that reason, Nelson C. Pierce Jr., an assistant usher in the White House, always
dreaded bringing Nancy her mail.

"She would get mad at me," Pierce says. "If her subscription was late or one of her friends in California had gotten the magazine and she hadn't, she would ask why she hadn't gotten hers." White House ushers would then be dispatched to search for the missing magazine at Washington newsstands, which invariably had not received their copies, either.

One afternoon Pierce brought Nancy her mail in the first family's west sitting room on the second floor of the White House. Nancy's dog Rex, a King Charles spaniel that was a Christmas gift from her husband, was lying at her feet.

Pierce was old friends with Rex, or so he thought. During the day, the usher's office — just inside the front entrance on the first floor of the mansion — is a favorite snoozing area for White House pets. But this time, for some reason, Rex was not at all cheerful about seeing Pierce. As Pierce turned to leave, Rex bit his ankle and held on. Pierce pointed his finger at the dog, a gesture to tell Nancy's pet to let go. But Nancy turned on Pierce.

"Don't you ever point a finger at my dog," she said.

Throughout his political life, Nancy stage-managed her husband.

"Did I ever give Ronnie advice? You bet I did," Nancy wrote in *My Turn: The Memoirs of Nancy Reagan*. "I'm the one who knows him best, and I was the only person in the White House who had absolutely no agenda of her own — except helping him."

"Mrs. Reagan was a precise and demanding woman," recalls John F. W. Rogers, the Reagan assistant and director of administration at the White House. "Her sole interest was the advancement of her husband's agenda."

In fact, most of Nancy's advice was sound. As she explained it, "As much as I love Ronnie, I'll admit he does have at least one fault: He can be naive about the people around him. Ronnie only tends to think well of people. While that's a fine quality in a friend, it can get you into trouble in politics."

Like Nancy, the Reagans' daughter Patti Davis was difficult. When agents were with her in New York, she would attempt to ditch them by jumping out of the Secret Service car while it was stopped in traffic. She viewed her detail as an annoyance.

"On one visit to New York City, she was with movie actor Peter Strauss, whom she was dating at the time," a former agent says. "Ms. Davis started to engage in the same tricks as on her previous visits and in general treated the assigned agent with disrespect. Strauss became incensed at her actions and told her, 'You'd better start treating these agents with respect or I'm going back to L.A.' "

"Guess what," the agent says. "She started treating us better."

Former agent Clark Larsen remembers Patti yelling at him and another agent for following too closely. "She didn't want agents around, but she had to," Larsen says. "She didn't have a choice, unless her dad signed off on it, and he wasn't about to do that and leave her out exposed to either embarrass him or to have something bad happen to her."

"At least with the Nixon kids, they would all get together, but there was not a lot of affection shown with the Reagan kids," a former agent on the Nixon and Reagan details says. "With the Reagan kids, each had his or her own agenda, and then they didn't want anything to do with the other one. They never got together as a family. Ever."

Former agent Lloyd Bulman got to know Reagan's first wife, actress Jane Wyman, while protecting Maureen Reagan, the president's daughter with Wyman.

"Jane Wyman was really nice," Bulman says. "I'd go up to her penthouse suite with Maureen, and Maureen would go inside the penthouse, and pretty soon I'd be standing by the door, and a hand would come around the corner, and it was Jane Wyman," Bulman says. "She would grab me by the shoulder and pull me inside and say, 'Come in and have some lemonade or some food. You're just like part of the family.' "

In contrast, Nancy Reagan was so controlling that she objected when her husband kibitzed with Secret Service agents.

"Reagan was such a down-to-earth individual, easy to talk to," an agent says. "He was the great communicator. He wanted to be on friendly terms. He accepted people for what they were. His wife was just the opposite. If she saw that he was having a conversation with the agents, and it looked like they were good ol' boys, and he was laughing, she would call him away. She called the shots."

On the day Reagan left office, he and Nancy flew to Los Angeles on Air Force One. Bleachers had been set up near a hangar, and a wildly cheering crowd welcomed him as the University of Southern California band played.

"As he was standing there, one of the

185

USC guys took his Trojan helmet off," a Secret Service agent says. "He said, 'Mr. President!,' and threw his helmet to him. He saw it and caught it and put it on. The crowd went wild."

But Nancy Reagan leaned over to him and said, "Take that helmet off right now. You look like a fool."

"You saw a mood change," the agent says. "And he took it off. That went on all the time."

While Reagan and Nancy had a loving relationship, like any married couple they had occasional fights.

"They were very affectionate and would kiss," Air Force One chief steward Charles Palmer says of the Reagans. But they also got mad at each other over what they should eat and other small issues. Palmer says Nancy could push the president only so far.

"We were going into Alaska. She had put on everything she could put on," Palmer says. "She turned around and said, 'Where are your gloves?' He said, 'I'm not wearing my gloves.' She said, 'Oh, yes, you are.' He said he was not."

Reagan finally took the gloves, but he said he could not shake hands while he was wearing them. He said he would not put them on, and he didn't, Palmer says.

When they were at the ranch, the Reagans would ride horses together every day after lunch. In contrast to Joe Biden's instruction that they stay a mile behind him in Delaware, besides having the military aide with the nuclear football with him on horseback, Reagan had the White House doctor follow him with Secret Service agents in a Humvee, former agent Patrick Sullivan says.

Despite his hard-riding cowboy roles in westerns, Reagan rode English, in breeches and boots. He usually rode El Alamein, a gray Anglo-Arab that former president José López Portillo of Mexico had given him.

"He would go up to the barn just outside the house, he would saddle up the horses, get them all ready, then he had one of those triangle bells," former agent Dennis Chomicki says. "He would always bang on that iron triangle, and that was Nancy Reagan's sign that the horses are ready, come on out, let's go."

One afternoon, Reagan was banging away on the bell, but Nancy did not appear. Finally, Reagan went in the house to get her. He came out with her, looking distressed. Then a technician from the White House Communications Agency told Chomicki that he had detected a problem with the ranch's phone system. A telephone set must be off the hook, he said, and the technician wanted to check on it. Chomicki allowed him to enter the Reagan home, and he soon came out holding a phone that had been smashed to pieces.

"She was on the phone," Chomicki says. "That's why she didn't come up to the barn. Nancy never really liked the ranch. She would go up there because the president liked it. Other than the ride, she used to stay in the house almost all the time, and a good portion of the time she'd be talking to her friends down in L.A. For the president," Chomicki says, "the highlight of his day was to go riding with Nancy. And when she didn't come out because she was talking on the phone, he threw the phone on the floor."

Nancy Reagan tried to restrict her husband's diet to healthy foods, but whenever she was not there, he reverted to his favorites.

"She was protective about what he ate," Air Force One steward Palmer remembers. "When she was not there, he ate differently. One of his favorite foods was macaroni and cheese. That was a no-no for her. If it was on the menu, she said, 'You're not eating that.'"

While most recent presidents liked their steak medium rare, Reagan liked his well done. He also liked hamburger soup — made with ground beef, tomatoes, and carrots — roast beef hash, beef and kidney pie, and osso buco. Nancy Reagan liked paella à la Valenciana, salmon mousse, and chicken pot pie. For dessert, the Reagans both liked apple brown Betty, prune whip, fruit with Cointreau, and plum pudding.

For all the spin from the Carter White House about not drinking, it was the Reagans who drank the least. During Reagan's years in office, on Air Force One, "I may have served the Reagans four drinks, maybe, with the exception of a glass of wine," Palmer says.

"Nancy Reagan was very protective of that guy," says Jimmy R. Bull, the chief communicator on Air Force One. "The president would need forty hours a day to do all the things people wanted him to do. You can run him into the ground in a hurry, mentally and physically."

"No one looked out for his welfare more or was more concerned about him as a human being," says James F. Kuhn, Reagan's administrative assistant during his second term. "Everyone said she was demanding. I remember her saying some things to me about things that should be done. But she never asked for anything for herself. It was always for her 'roommate,' as she called him."

15
CORNER CUTTING

On the spur of the moment, Vice President Joe Biden decided one evening to attend a gathering of community activists at a church in a dangerous, crime-ridden urban neighborhood. Drug deals were being made openly on street corners there, and gunshots could be heard in the area. When a Secret Service agent told a local police officer about the plan, he looked at him as if he were crazy.

Still, agents obliged. Since this would be what agents refer to as an "off-the-record movement," meaning no advance notice goes out that the protectee is attending, agents did not insist on setting up stand-alone magnetometers. But they did insist on screening each participant for weapons with handheld magnetometers.

Soon, a line formed as the screening by the agents delayed entrance to the late evening meeting. At that point, one of

Biden's staffers told an agent on the detail that Biden wanted the screening stopped.

"The vice president doesn't want to see these people lined up," the staffer yelled.

The agent explained the need for hand-magging: Anyone with a weapon could decide to take out the vice president. The agent suggested that the staffer leave security decisions to the Secret Service.

Unappeased, the staffer then called a Secret Service supervisor, who overruled the agent at the scene: Agents could search every other person in line. It left open the possibility that someone with a weapon could get a shot at the vice president. According to a witness to the conversation, in ordering the detail leader on the scene to cease screening everyone, the Secret Service supervisor, who was black, essentially accused the agent of being racist, insinuating that the agent had called for everyone to be screened because the participants at the meeting were black.

Secret Service agents say this kind of corner cutting and high-handed undercutting of basic security rules is par for the course. The corner cutting and laxness began in 2003 when the Secret Service moved from the Treasury Department to the Department of Homeland Security.

Forced to compete for funds with twenty-one other national security agencies in a department that has 240,000 employees, the Secret Service became more political and compliant. Mark Sullivan, who was appointed director by President George W. Bush in 2006, proudly proclaimed that the Secret Service "makes do with less."

Like all Secret Service directors, Sullivan came up through the ranks. He was highly regarded as an agent. But when it came to managing the agency, he was in denial about the wide gap between the image of invincibility the Secret Service likes to project and the reality.

The most egregious example of the corner cutting is that on a regular basis, when staffs of the president, vice president, or presidential candidates apply pressure, Secret Service agents comply with management's wishes and allow people into events without magnetometer screening. That is akin to letting passengers onto a jetliner without passing them through magnetometers.

Anyone who allowed a passenger onto an airliner without going through a magnetometer would be fired and possibly prosecuted. But Andy Card, President George W. Bush's former chief of staff, tells me Secret Service management assures the White House staff that stopping screening is not a problem. The White House trusts the service and its claim that it offers "layers of protection."

Aides want to believe in the omnipotence of the Secret Service because it serves their political ends: They want presidents to be accessible to the public and don't want to annoy supporters with inconvenient security measures that lead to delays. Yet if one of the people allowed through without screening drew a weapon or threw a grenade and assassinated a president or a candidate, it would be entirely because of the Secret Service's negligence.

An agent who was on Obama's presidential candidate detail says it was "not uncommon" to waive magnetometer screening at events when the crowd was larger than expected. While the overflow might be seated far from the candidate and often behind a buffer zone, "someone could still fire a gun, make their way to the front, or detonate explosives," the agent says.

Other agents say magnetometers have also been waived for events attended by President George W. Bush and every recent leading presidential candidate. Agents attribute such blatant lapses in security to the fact that the Secret Service does not have enough manpower to screen everyone properly.

"At major events, we are typically understaffed, and in order to appease staff, senior Secret Service management on the president's or vice president's detail under pressure simply orders us to open up the magnetometers — just open them up, let them through," a current agent says. "On any given day, it is acceptable to senior management to open up screening and compromise security."

"It's complacency," says an agent who was on Obama's detail. "They say we can make do with less."

Shutting down magnetometers as an event is about to start is shocking enough. But when Vice President Biden threw the opening pitch at the first Baltimore Orioles game of the season at Camden Yards on April 6, 2009, the Secret Service had not screened with magnetometers any of the more than forty thousand fans. Moreover, even though Biden's scheduled attendance at the game had been announced beforehand, the vice president was not wearing a bulletproof vest under his navy sport shirt as he stood on the pitcher's mound.

According to an agent, before the Baltimore event, senior management on Biden's detail decided "we don't need magnetometers," overruling stunned agents on Biden's detail and in the agency's Baltimore field office.

"A gunman or gunmen from anywhere in the stands could have gotten off multiple rounds before we could have gotten in the line of fire," says a current agent who is outraged that the Secret Service would be so reckless.

Referring to the decision to dispense with magnetometer screening, an agent says, "The Secret Service has dismantled the first line of defense against an assassination. They can say it's okay, but it will not be okay when the president or vice president is killed."

When confronted with examples of corner cutting, Secret Service management takes a dismissive, blasé attitude. In his office on the ninth floor of Secret Service headquarters, Nicholas Trotta, who headed the Office of Protective Operations, talks about lessons learned from previous assassinations and assassination attempts. After the attempt on President Reagan's life, "we expanded our use of the magnetometers." Now, he says, "everyone goes through the magnetometer."

Often, just seeing a magnetometer in use

is a deterrent, Trotta notes. But what about instances when the Secret Service buckles under pressure from campaign personnel or White House staff to let people into events without being screened? Not prepared for this question, Trotta tries to backtrack and change his story.

"When we have a crowd of seventy thousand people, we may or may not need to put all those people through magnetometers," Trotta says. "Because some of those people in certain areas might not have a line-of-sight threat that can harm the protectee."

But what if an assassination occurred because someone was not screened? Trotta looks uncomfortable. Still, he plows on ahead, saying a lot of factors come into play.

"The president can go to a sports arena or stadium and may stay in a box," Trotta says. "Let's say if he's on the third base side up in a box, the people on the first base side, center field, they might not be the threat. But the people around him may be the threat. So now we screen that area, and the critical part is to make sure that there's no handoff, so you have a dead space that is secure."

Buffers or not, has Trotta never heard of an assassin leaving his seat to zip off a shot or to throw a grenade at the president? In fact, it was a decision to stop magnetometer screening that almost led to the assassination of President George W. Bush on May 10, 2005. That was when a man threw a grenade at him as he spoke at a rally in a public square in Tbilisi, Georgia. Because magnetometer screening had been stopped by local authorities, the man was able to take a grenade into the event where Bush was to speak.

The grenade landed near the podium where the president was speaking, but it did not explode. Later, witnesses said a man wearing a head scarf and standing off to the side had reached into his black leather jacket and pulled out a military grenade. He yanked the pin, wrapped the scarf around the grenade, and threw it toward Bush.

Inside a grenade, the chemical reaction that creates an explosion occurs when two spoons disengage. But because the spoons got stuck when the grenade landed, no explosion occurred. After analyzing the device, the FBI concluded that it could have killed the president. If all onlookers had been screened, the grenade would have been detected, and Bush's life would not have been in jeopardy.

Prior to that attack, the assassination of Senator Robert F. Kennedy and the attempts on the lives of Presidents Reagan and Ford and Governor George Wallace could have been prevented if bystanders had been screened with magnetometers.

When told of Trotta's rationale for stopping magnetometer screening, Secret Service agents cannot believe he said what he did indeed say.

"I was in absolute shock regarding his comment about the mags closing down and potential attackers being too far away to cause any problems," says an agent on one of the two major protective details. Imagine, the agent says, if three or four suicide assassins came in with guns firing.

"Saying not everyone in a seventy-thousand-person event is close enough to shoot the protectee is an amazing answer," says another agent on one of the major protective details. "I'm embarrassed that an assistant director would give you that answer."

Danny Defenbaugh, a former FBI agent who publicly criticized the Secret Service's decision to stop magnetometer screening at an Obama campaign event in Dallas, notes that word can quickly spread that the agency engages in such lax practices.

"The people who want to assassinate the president will watch and look for the Secret Service to close down the magnetometers before an event starts," he says.

Trotta's cavalier responses are symptomatic of the Secret Service's refusal to acknowledge or address problems that undermine the agency's mission. The laxness begins with the Secret Service's most basic responsibility: to provide agents with weapons that will protect them and the president.

At the Rowley center, the Secret Service likes to impress members of Congress with agents' marksmanship. But what the agency doesn't tell Congress, according to agents, is how they are outgunned because the Secret Service continues to use the outdated Heckler & Koch MP5 submachine gun. In contrast, the Army and other federal law enforcement agencies have switched to the newer and more powerful Colt M4 carbine.

While a counterassault team travels with the president and is armed with the SR-16 — similar to the M4 — other agents on a protective detail also need to be ready to repel an attack. Many of those agents are equipped only with the MP5. In addition, all agents are armed with a SIG Sauer P229 pistol with the barrel modified to accommodate a .357 round instead of the standard smaller nine-millimeter round.

"The service, you would think, would be on the leading edge when it comes to weapons, and they're just not," says a current agent. "They're still carrying MP5 submachine guns," developed in the 1960s. He notes that the State Department's Diplomatic Security agents and U.S. soldiers overseas are armed with the M4. Developed in the 1990s, it is "much more powerful. It has better range and better armor-piercing capabilities," the agent adds.

The Army uses the M4 as its main weapon. The FBI trains agents to use both the MP5 and the M4. Even the Amtrak Police Department is equipped with the M4.

"You're going to be getting attacked with AK-47 assault rifles, you're going to be getting attacked with M4s," an agent says. "We want to be able to match or better whoever's attacking us. You want to get the same range or better. The problem is if you're getting a shoot-out in a motorcade, with the MP5, you're shooting a pistol with a submachine gun round — you're basically shooting a pistol round. You don't want your rounds falling short and not even able to reach out to the bad guy. And that's essentially what you've got going on with the weapons they have now."

16
"KEEP YOUR HEAD DOWN"

Secret Service agents breathed a collective sigh of relief when George H. W. Bush took office. Unlike previous presidents, such as Lyndon Johnson and Jimmy Carter, Bush treated agents with respect and consideration.

Bush "made it clear to all his staff that none of them was a security expert, and if the Secret Service made a decision, he was the one to sign off on it, and they were never to question our decisions or make life difficult," former agent Pete Dowling says. "So consequently it was kind of a moment in time, because all the entities really worked well together to make his protection and the activities that he participated in successful."

Like Ronald Reagan, Bush was so considerate of the agents who protected him that he would stay in town on Christmas Eve so agents could spend it with their families.

Then he would fly to Texas the day after Christmas.

"Bush is a great man, just an all-around nice person," an agent says. "Both he and Mrs. Bush are very thoughtful, and they think outside their own little world. They think of other people."

"Bush understands that politics is politics and friendship is friendship," an agent who was on his detail says. "He can be friends with a lot of people who may not agree with him. The only things that bothered him were things that were important to the country. Little things just kind of seemed to roll off of him."

When Bush — code-named Timberwolf — was vice president, agent William Albracht was on the midnight shift at the vice president's residence. While agents refer to the President's Protective Detail as the Show, they call the Vice President's Protective Detail the Little Show with Free Parking. That's because, unlike the White House, the vice president's residence provides parking for agents.

Albracht was new to the post, and Agent Dowling filled him in.

"Well, Bill, every day the stewards bake the cookies, and that is their job, and that is their responsibility," Dowling told him.

"And then our responsibility on midnights is to find those cookies or those left from the previous day and eat as many of them as possible."

Assigned to the basement post around 3 A.M., Albracht was getting hungry.

"We never had permission to take food from the kitchen, but sometimes you get very hungry on midnights," Albracht says. "I walked into the kitchen that was located in the basement and opened up the refrigerator. I'm hoping that there are some leftover snacks from that day's reception," the former agent says. "It was slim pickin's. All of a sudden, there's a voice over my shoulder."

"Hey, anything good in there to eat?" the man asked.

"No, looks like they cleaned it out," Albracht said.

"I turned around to see George Bush off my right shoulder," Albracht says. "After I get over the shock of who it was, Bush says, 'Hey, I was really hoping there would be something to eat.' And I said, 'Well, sir, every day the stewards bake cookies, but every night they hide them from us.' With a wink of his eye he says, 'Let's find 'em.' So we tore the kitchen apart, and sure enough we did find them. He took a stack of chocolate chip cookies and a glass of milk and went back up to bed, and I took a stack and a glass of milk and went back to the basement post."

When Albracht returned to the post, Dowling asked, "Who the hell were you in there talking to?"

Albracht told him what had happened. "Oh yeah, sure, right," Dowling said.

When he was vice president, Bush flew to a fund-raiser in Boise, Idaho, during the 1982 election campaign. He was to have dinner at the Chart House seafood restaurant on North Garden Street, on the banks of the Boise River.

"The way we protected him, we had some agents inside, but typically what we'd do was situate ourselves at dining tables near him," Dowling says.

Dowling had been seated for a few minutes when he heard a radio transmission: Two white males in camouflage outfits and carrying long weapons were creeping around the back toward their location. They were crawling on their bellies, moving themselves along with their elbows.

Just then, Dowling looked up and saw the two bad guys. He thought of intelligence reports that Libya had sent a hit squad to the United States to kill American officials.

The agent instinctively jumped out of his chair and tackled Bush to protect him. Food flew everywhere as Dowling threw the vice president on the ground and flopped on top of him.

"What's going on here?" Bush demanded to know.

"I don't know, but just keep your head down," Dowling answered.

Dowling looked up. He saw dozens of law enforcement officers with their guns drawn — Secret Service agents, sheriff's department deputies, and state troopers. They were on the scene as part of routine protection for a vice presidential visit. The two bad guys were kneeling with their hands clasped behind their heads.

"We evacuated the VP out of the restaurant to get him away from whatever danger may have still been there," Dowling says. "You would think I had just thwarted an assassination attempt."

As it turned out, the restaurant was near an apartment complex where the girlfriend of one of the two men lived.

"The guy had gone to see his girlfriend, and she was there with another guy," Dowling says. "So the boyfriend got very angry. The other guy who was there with his girlfriend pulled out a knife, kind of slashed him, didn't hurt him badly. So this fellow who had been cut decided that he and another guy were going to go back and kill the guy that night."

Not knowing the vice president was coming, they parked in the lot at the Chart House and decided to sneak through the woods to get to the apartment complex. They were tried and convicted on illegal weapons and attempted assault charges.

Agents noted the contrast between George H. W. Bush and Al Gore, Bush's successor as vice president. Like Hillary Clinton, Gore — who also claimed to be a champion of the little people — treated agents with disdain and told them he did not want to be bothered greeting them or seeing them.

"Gore told agents at his home in Carthage, Tennessee, that they should duck behind bushes when they rotated shifts because the Gores didn't want to see them," a former agent says.

"I was on the detail one Christmas when Gore was at his home in Carthage," former agent Jeff Crane says. "Neighbors offered us food on Christmas Day, but the Gores never even bothered to say 'Merry Christmas' or 'Thank you.' "

Every agent has heard the story of how

Gore was bawling out his son Al Gore III over poor performance at school and warned him, "If you don't straighten up, you won't get into the right schools, and if you don't get into the right schools, you could end up like these guys."

Gore — code-named Sundance — motioned toward the agents protecting him.

"Sometimes Gore would come out of the residence, get in the car, and he wouldn't even give the guys the coachman's nod. Nothing," a former agent says. "It was like we didn't exist. We were only there to facilitate him to get from point A to point B." As professionals, the agent says, "we do not have to like you to protect you, but it can make the long hours a bit more tolerable."

Like Bill Clinton, Gore was perpetually late.

"The schedule would call for him to leave the vice president's residence at 7:15 A.M.," former agent Dave Saleeba says. "At 7:30 A.M., we would check on him, and he would be eating a muffin at the pool."

Gore would exit the vice president's residence late for an appointment at the White House, climb in the Secret Service limousine, and say to agents, "Could you speed it up, but don't use the lights and sirens? Get me there as fast as you can."

The Secret Service was not about to speed in traffic without lights and sirens. But agents quickly came up with a solution.

"The special agent in charge would come on the radio and say, 'Yeah, let's move as quick as we can but safely,' " former agent Dennis Chomicki says. "He'd do it just for the entertainment of the vice president."

Without pressing the button to transmit, another agent would say into the microphone, "Hey, let's go, speed it up," Chomicki says. "That would satisfy Gore in the backseat."

Gore had "really poor manners," Chomicki says. "He used to pass gas in the car, and he could care less. He had no class whatsoever."

Having the habit of never carrying money, Gore would borrow from agents when necessary. "I think he always thought, I'm the vice president, I don't have to pay for anything," Chomicki says.

Unlike Gore, Bush 41, as he is called, never took agents for granted or imposed on them. But like many presidents, he chafed at protection.

"Most people have difficulty adjusting to having protection," says former Secret Service deputy director Danny Spriggs.

"These folks do it because it goes with the job. However, it's nothing they embrace initially. You infringe on their private lives. Even though I did it for twenty-eight years, I can't imagine what it would be like to be told I can't go to a movie or amusement park whenever I want, or to be told that friends I have known for years must submit their name, Social Security number, and date of birth before they can visit me."

Despite warnings from his detail, Bush would insist on leaving the Oval Office through the door to the Rose Garden and greeting tourists lined up along the fence on Pennsylvania Avenue. Bush's detail leader assigned agents to rush to the fence as soon as an alarm notified them that Bush had opened the door to the outside. Soon, the *Washington Post* ran a story reporting that tourists were delighted at their unexpected encounter with the president. Just after that, agents spotted what Agent Glenn Smith calls a "textbook" possible assassin as Bush was greeting onlookers at the fence.

"The man had on a coat in the summer, he looked disheveled, and his eyes were darting in all directions," Smith recalls. "We patted him down, and it turned out he had a nine-millimeter pistol on him and probably intended to use it on the president."

After that, the detail leader had a talk with Bush. He pointed out to the president that by greeting people spontaneously, he was endangering not only himself but his agents. From then on, "Bush would give us time to set up a secure zone at the fence," Smith says.

At one point, Bush and his wife, Barbara, were staying at their Kennebunkport home in the winter, and they went out for a walk in the freezing cold.

"I had a hat on, and two of the other agents had a hat on, but the one agent assigned to the first lady didn't bring a hat with him," says former agent Patrick F. Sullivan, who was on the President's Protective Detail from 1986 to 1990. "So the president came out with Mrs. Bush, and we started to walk."

"Where's your hat?" Mrs. Bush asked the hatless agent.

"Oh, Mrs. Bush, I didn't bring one. I didn't realize it was going to be so cold here," he said.

"George, we need to get this agent a hat," Barbara Bush — code-named Tranquillity — said.

"Okay, Bar," he replied.

She walked back into the house, got one of President Bush's furry hats, and gave it to the agent.

"No, Mrs. Bush, that's fine," the agent said.

"Hey, don't argue with Mrs. Bush," Bush said.

The agent put on the president's hat.

"That was Mrs. Bush," Sullivan says. "She was everyone's mother, and she didn't want this forty-year-old man walking around at Kennebunkport without a hat on. She was a sweetheart."

"Barbara and George Bush were genuinely in love," Albracht says. "They share a special bond of being married and being each other's best friend that you don't really see a lot of."

Today Bush's memory is fading, but agents say he and Barbara are as considerate of them as ever. When the two-year-old son of one of the agents on his protective detail lost his hair after being treated for leukemia, to show his support for the boy, Bush followed the lead of the agents by having his head shaved. He also donated to a fund to help defray the boy's medical costs.

"When little Patrick got leukemia, a lot of the agents shaved their heads, and I said why not me?" Bush said in an NBC interview with his granddaughter Jenna Bush Hager. "It was the right thing to do."

17
HAWKEYE

A female Secret Service agent on the president's detail is so out of shape that she literally cannot open the heavy doors to exit the president's limousine. Instead of removing her from protecting the president and requiring her to pass the physical fitness tests that all agents are supposed to take every three months, Secret Service management told drivers to try to park the Beast so it would be easier for the vehicle door to swing open for her.

If the president were shot, she could not help carry him to safety, an agent notes. Agents know there is no point in complaining to a supervisor: The overweight female agent is a supervisor.

Secret Service management condones the same sort of corner cutting and favoritism when it comes to evaluations for promotion. They have become so meaningless that agents are actually handed blank forms and

asked to evaluate themselves on their quali-
fications for promotion and how they scored
on physical fitness tests. According to
agents, those who have "juice" or "hooks"
with management because they play golf
with someone get promoted regardless of
their merit.

"Forget physical fitness tests," says a
recently retired agent. "We are not given
the time to do them."

"You are supposed to do your physical
training test quarterly, but I haven't done
one in two, three years," an agent says.
"When you do, you enter your scores your-
self on a form and hand it in." In fact, the
agent says, "I'm one of the PT instructors.
And because the service takes physical
training so lightly, I don't take it seriously
either. Just give me a sheet, and I trust that
what the agent says he did is accurate."

"There is a policy in place that you have
to maintain a certain physical fitness standard every quarter, but it's more like an
agent fabricates his or her sheet and hands
it to a fitness coordinator," another agent
says. "I'm a fitness coordinator, and I enter
the phony scores."

As a result, agents say, many of their colleagues are out of shape.

"Some of them, you just roll your eyes,"

an agent says. "One agent cannot even do a sit-up. I know for a fact he can't because his belly's already up to his chin. Just look at some of the details, and you can really see where the standards have gone — downhill."

"We had a post stander, a female agent, and I was in shock," says an agent, referring to agents assigned temporarily to guard a specific area or site. "Overweight, out of shape, just disgusting. And you look at this person and say, 'If I'm going to go through a door with you to execute a search warrant, are you going to have my back? If I get shot, are you going to be able to carry me out? Or are you going to be able to get up four flights of stairs because I'm in a fight with somebody?' Probably not."

While the Secret Service has been ignoring its own fitness requirements and letting spectators into events without magnetometer screening, it has also been cutting back on the size of counterassault teams. For the sake of cosmetics, the Secret Service bows to demands of staff that the teams remain at a distance from protectees.

Outside the White House, the counterassault team, or CAT, is critical to providing protection. A heavily armed tactical unit, it is assigned to the president, vice president, foreign heads of state, or any other protectee deemed to require extra coverage, like a presidential candidate. In the event of an attack, CAT's mission is to divert the attack from a protectee, allowing the working shift of agents to shield and evacuate the individual. Once the "problem" is dealt with, CAT members regroup, and the shift leader directs them on their next move.

The Secret Service began using counter-assault teams on a limited basis in 1979. They were formed after several agents involved in training were talking over lunch and began to speculate on how the Secret Service would deal with a terrorist attack, according to Taylor Rudd, one of the agents. After President Reagan was shot in 1981, the teams were expanded and centralized at headquarters in 1983.

CAT differs from a special weapons and tactics team (SWAT), which the police or Secret Service may deploy once an attack has occurred. Code-named Hawkeye, CAT takes action as the attack occurs and remains until the threat is contained or neutralized.

Clad in black battle-dress uniforms known as BDUs, CAT members travel with the president. They are trained in close-quarters battle — when small units engage the enemy with weapons at very close range. They are also trained in motorcade ambush tactics.

Each CAT team member is equipped with a semiautomatic Stoner SR-16 rifle, a SIG Sauer P229 pistol, flash-bang grenades for diversionary tactics, and smoke grenades. CAT agents also may be armed with a Remington breaching shotgun, a weapon that has been modified with a short barrel. The shotgun may be loaded with nonlethal Hatton rounds to blow the lock off a door.

In contrast to the CAT team, the counter-sniper team, whose members also wear black BDUs, does not travel in the motor-cade. Instead, the countersnipers — code-named Hercules and long used by the Secret Service — take positions at key exit and entrance points. For instance, when the president is leaving or entering the White House, they position themselves on the roof and on balconies across the street. Counter-snipers are required to qualify by shooting at ranges up to a thousand yards each month. If they don't qualify, they don't travel or work.

In another example of cutting corners, for presidential candidates and many protect-ees below the president and vice president, counterassault teams have been slashed in the past several years from the requisite five to six agents to only two agents. Given their training, that renders the teams almost useless, agents say.

"A CAT is trained to operate as a full team of five to six men," a current agent who was formerly on CAT says. "Each member has a specific function based upon the direction of the attack. A two-man element responds to the problem, while another responds to the attack with a base of fire — providing cover fire and trying to suppress the attackers — while the other element moves on them to destroy them. The other two-man element — or solo member if there are only five operators — provides coverage in the rear and assists the element that is moving to address the attack."

A team of only two men "cannot do all of those tasks, on top of communicating to the protective detail a status report detailing number of attackers, number of good guys or bad guys killed or captured, and then requesting direction from the detail leader about the next course of action," the agent says.

"Using two CAT members rather than the full team provides a false sense of security and is a tremendous misuse of a very important tactical asset," William Albracht, who trained new agents, says.

Secret Service rules require agents based in Washington to qualify with a pistol once a month and with long guns every three months. But, in contrast to years past, many agents find they are given time to take the qualifying test for long guns only once or twice a year.

"I've had conversations with special agents in charge who say they are not able to get the requalification training in they would like because of the operational demands they have," says Spriggs, who retired from the Secret Service as deputy director in 2004. In previous years, "we never sacrificed training," he says.

Dishonesty should not be tolerated in any law enforcement agency. Yet when the Secret Service wows members of Congress with supposedly unrehearsed feats that bring down the bad guys and save the lives of protectees at the Rowley Training Center, it pretends that the scenarios are spontaneous. In fact, they are secretly rehearsed beforehand.

"Members of Congress were being escorted around the training complex, and we were doing building extraction scenarios with the protectee," an agent recalls. "We would be trying to move the VP out of a hotel. Say there's a fire in the hotel, or there's an explosion outside. We want to get him down into the motorcade and out of the area and move him to a secure location."

On this particular morning when members of Congress were due to visit, "everything changed," the agent says. "Everything was rehearsed, everything was put together, and we're like why are we doing rehearsed scenarios? We should be doing practical scenarios and real training exercises."

The agents were told, "Well, there's a congressional tour coming through."

Normally, in a training exercise, "the bad guy can kill the agent," the agent says. "You don't know. You could see the agent get killed, you could see two agents stumble over each other down a stairwell, things could happen. If you're putting on training that's effective, it is a practical exercise in the sense you let it run through to its end. But when the congressional tour came through, we did it as we had rehearsed to do it," the agent says. In real training, "you never rehearse something like that."

The rehearsed scenario did the trick, impressing the senators and representatives who watched. "They watched an attack on a principal and saw how agents responded, how the shift goes to the protectee, how the

CAT team deploys. But they didn't know that they spent the last couple days rehearsing that scenario," an agent notes.

According to another current agent, the same thing happened when the Secret Service opened the Rowley center to a group of visiting U.S. attorneys. Prior to their visit, like kids rehearsing a school play, the agents rehearsed scenarios for two hours.

That is not the way it's supposed to happen. In real training, "you know what the setting is, that the president will give a speech," former Secret Service deputy director Spriggs says. "They are not told what will happen. They don't know if an attack will come, where it will come from, or what it will be."

The Secret Service engages in the same kind of dishonesty when it pads arrest statistics proudly presented to Congress and the public. In fiscal 2011, the Secret Service made 9,022 arrests for financial crimes, according to its annual report. But that figure includes arrests that the agency never made. They are so-called in-custody responses, which means the Secret Service takes credit for an arrest when local police notify the agency that they have a suspect in custody for the equivalent of a counterfeiting violation or other financial crime.

"When you are a field agent, you are strongly urged to call the local police departments in your district and have them contact you if they made an arrest, state or local," a veteran agent says. "Then you write up the necessary reports and claim credit for the arrest and conviction of the subject."

"The reason they do it obviously is so they can walk over to Congress and inflate the investigative success of the agency," says a former agent who left the Secret Service to join the inspector general's office of another federal agency. "They make a copy of the police report and make a copy of the note, and that's about it. The FBI does not do that. It's a game, and it's deceptive."

Secret Service spokesman Edwin Donovan did not respond when asked for comment on the practice of padding arrest statistics and secretly rehearsing threat scenarios.

Each point of the Secret Service star emblazoned on special agents' badges represents one of the agency's five core values: justice, duty, courage, honesty, and loyalty. But too often, honesty is missing from Secret Service management's way of doing business.

18
ENERGIZER

Like his wife, Bill Clinton has an explosive temper that he directs at aides, calling them "stupid" and "morons."

"If he was in a hurry, Clinton would literally push staff out of his way," an agent says. "He could turn on you instantly."

Secret Service agents call it "Clinton Standard Time" — a reference to Clinton's usual practice of running one to two hours late. To Clinton, an itinerary with scheduled appointments is merely "a suggestion," a former agent says.

Clinton was "always late for everything," an agent on Clinton's detail says. "He could be in his room playing cards. We would stay waiting for him for an hour because he was playing Hearts with his staff."

"Bill Clinton was never on time," former agent Jeff Crane says. "He didn't care how late he was or whether it strained our resources. But Bush 41 [George H. W.

Bush] was so apologetic if he was late, it was almost embarrassing. He hated to inconvenience us."

According to Jane Burka, coauthor of *Procrastination,* such behavior is often a tool of control. "In effect, they [tardy people] are saying, 'I'm in control. I run on my own schedule,' " she says. These people are "oblivious to the needs of others — they get so self-absorbed they literally lose track of time."

In contrast, Clinton managed to be on time for most of his assignations with Gennifer Flowers in Arkansas.

"I don't recall him being real late," Flowers tells me. "I can recall things coming up, and he would call me. He would say he would call me later. He never did not show up."

Air Force One tends to bring out the true character of presidents. In command of their own flying carpet and confined to a small space over many hours, presidents who are arrogant and haughty tend to exhibit those traits more. Bill Clinton's escapades on Air Force One were prime examples.

In May 1993, Clinton ordered the presidential plane to wait on the tarmac at Los Angeles International Airport while he got a haircut from Christophe Schatteman, a Beverly Hills hairdresser. Schatteman's clients have included Nicole Kidman, Goldie Hawn, and Steven Spielberg.

"We flew out of San Diego to L.A. to pick him up," recalls James Saddler, a steward on the infamous trip. "Some guy came out and said he was supposed to cut the president's hair. Christophe cut his hair, and we took off. We were on the ground for an hour. They closed the runways."

While Christophe cut Clinton's hair, two runways at LAX were closed. That meant all incoming and outgoing flights had to be halted. Clinton's thoughtlessness inconvenienced passengers throughout the country.

Like a teenager, Clinton would exchange observations with male crew members about the anatomy of any attractive woman who happened to be on the plane. To female crew members, he would make off-color remarks.

Howard Franklin, the chief Air Force One steward, told Clinton's advance people that "the key to being effective was planning." That novel idea brought a vigorous retort. "They said, 'We got here by being spontaneous, and we're not going to change,' " Franklin recalls. Besides an aversion to planning, Clinton and his staff brought with them the attitude that "the military were people who couldn't get jobs," Franklin notes.

Despite his flaws, when away from Hillary, Clinton, when he was president, he would occasionally go out of his way to be friendly to agents and uniformed officers.

"Bill Clinton would come out on the South Lawn at ten o'clock at night, smoke a cigar, and he'd start talking to you," says a former uniformed officer. "At the time my wife was pregnant, and like two or three months later he came out on the South Lawn and walked up, lit up a cigar, and asked me how my wife was doing. And you know, I was just a Uniformed Division guy. That was pretty impressive."

When Clinton was away from the White House, agents were always concerned because he would spot a pretty woman and make a beeline for her.

"Clinton was going to a retreat in Williamsburg, Virginia," an agent who was temporarily on his detail recalls. "The standard operating procedure was, at all costs, keep women out of the arrival point area, because he will make a beeline to them. That was my job: Make sure there's no women in eyesight of him, because if he sees a pretty woman, he'll walk over there out in the open and will be exposed. Other people will want to come over and see him and speak to him. So it was a security concern."

When Clinton was to shake hands with onlookers, bored agents amused themselves by scoping out which attractive woman he might zero in on. Standing near one of them at the rope line, an agent would radio to fellow agents, "Wouldja?" — meaning "Would you do her?" Then he would say, "Would he?" To signify they thought Clinton would, other agents would press the button on their microphones twice. The double clicking in their earpieces meant yes. When a knockout young woman was the object of this game, "you would hear a cacophony of clicks," says a former agent on Clinton's detail.

When Clinton flew to Fresno, California, "we had a chain-link fence set up to keep the crowds back at the airport," former agent Cliff Baranowski says. "I had a special section for Secret Service employees and their families. He got off Air Force One, and he walked to the crowd area. He sees this blond lady, and he kisses her on the lips. It turned out to be another agent's wife. She was thrilled that he picked her out. But I couldn't believe it."

Clinton loved greeting people and had a

gift for remembering their names. After a speech in New York at an AFL-CIO convention, he was shaking hands. Agents noticed a busboy eyeing him and moving closer.

"Clinton saw him and called him by his name," says an agent on his detail at the time. "The president shook his hand and asked how his father was. The busboy got teary-eyed and said his father had died. Commiserating with him, Clinton turned to an aide and said the man's father had had cancer."

The Secret Service tried to adapt to Clinton's unpredictable style.

"President Clinton would see a small crowd of spectators that may have gathered behind a rope outside our secure perimeter just to get a glimpse of the president, and he would head off to shake their hands," says former agent Norm Jarvis. "Of course, this drove us to distraction because we didn't want him to approach an un-magged crowd. We didn't know if we had a Hinckley or Bremer in the crowd with a handgun," he added, referring to Arthur Bremer, who shot Governor George Wallace of Alabama when Wallace was campaigning for president. "A person like that might be loitering in the area because he couldn't get into the event."

At one point, Jarvis was faced with just such a situation: Clinton plunged spontaneously into a crowd that had not been screened. Jarvis was in the lead on the rope line and noticed a woman with her hands under her coat.

During an event, "you'll be in the formation and walking along with the president, you spot something, and you say something over the air to the shift leader," Jarvis says. "You're generally very quiet. There's not a lot of chatter, but if you say something and you're with the president, it means something. You size up the person that causes you to bring your attention to them and you have to make a quick judgment as to what you're going to do or what the detail needs to do."

In this case, "what was strange was everyone was looking at the president — clapping, yelling, smiling," Jarvis says. "She was staring down and had a real puzzled look on her face. Mind you, the president was two arms' lengths from us. I let the shift leader know I had a problem, and I just wrapped my arms around this woman because I didn't have time to frisk her."

Jarvis held her in a bear hug as the shift and the president worked their way around him.

"She was startled, but I wouldn't let her arms out from under the coat," Jarvis says. "I held her until I could get some assistance, which arrived from a protective intelligence team that was nearby."

The team interviewed the woman and quickly determined that she was mentally ill.

"She didn't have a weapon under her coat, but you can tell mentally disturbed people by the way they react," Jarvis notes. "And when they react the opposite of everybody else, it brings your attention to them, and you know you've got an issue out of the ordinary."

At one point during his second term, agents say Clinton managed to lose the plastic authenticator card with the codes he would need to verify his identity to launch nuclear weapons.

"He has to keep those codes with him at all times, at all costs," says a former agent. "With the codes, the White House Communications Agency can set up communications through the nuclear football and hit the satellites."

Retired general Hugh Shelton, the former chairman of the Joint Chiefs of Staff, confirmed in his book *Without Hesitation: The Odyssey of an American Warrior* that in

Clinton's last year in office, the required codes for launching a nuclear strike were missing for months. "This is a big deal — a gargantuan deal — and we dodged a silver bullet," Shelton wrote.

As the Secret Service sees it, Hillary and Bill Clinton have a business relationship, not a marriage.

"They would talk on an encrypted phone," an agent says. "He would give her advice. It was a political alliance. My impression was they didn't have sex. She portrayed herself as devastated by the revelations of Monica [Lewinsky]. I doubt she cared." When Hillary was away, attractive women would show up at the White House residence late at night, former agents say.

While Secret Service agents and uniformed officers never observed Monica Lewinsky having sex with Clinton, they sensed that something was going on between them. For someone who worked in the West Wing, Lewinsky was over her head yet acted as if she owned the place. She would hug agents and act flirtatiously with them. Uniformed officers noticed her in the Oval Office pantry or private study, sometimes looking embarrassed that they had seen her.

On Easter Sunday, April 7, 1996, Clinton

was in the Oval Office at 4:56 P.M. Lewinsky told Secret Service agents she wanted to deliver some papers to him. After some time elapsed, Lewinsky had not left, and a White House operator told the Secret Service that Clinton was not answering his phone. Worried that something might have happened to the president, a Secret Service agent knocked on the door to the Oval Office. When he got no response, he entered and called out, "Mr. President?" Still no response.

The agent checked behind the desk and again called out, "Mr. President?" Then he noticed that the door to Clinton's study off the Oval Office was slightly ajar. According to Lewinsky, the president typically left the door to the study open while they were engaging in sex there. The agent called Clinton's name again. This time, the president responded and said he would pick up the phone if the call — which was from aide Dick Morris — was routed to his study.

According to the report of independent counsel Kenneth Starr, Lewinsky was giving Clinton oral sex at the time. After Clinton took the call, he told Lewinsky to continue as he talked politics with Morris. She obliged for the nine-minute duration of the call and left at 5:28 P.M.

The agent, who was not named in the Starr report, tells me jokingly that if he had pushed open the door to the study, "I either would have been fired or named Secret Service director."

On August 17, 1998, Bill Clinton stood in the Map Room of the White House and on national television confessed that he had lied about his relationship with Lewinsky. "Indeed, I did have a relationship with Miss Lewinsky that was not appropriate. In fact, it was wrong," Clinton said.

The next day, the president and Hillary flew to Martha's Vineyard.

"I was up at Martha's Vineyard right after he had confessed on national TV to the whole Monica Lewinsky affair," a former agent says. While the agent was operating the command post, Hillary called him and said, "Where is he?"

"Ma'am, the president is downtown right now, I think he just arrived at a Starbucks," the agent said.

"Confirm that," Hillary demanded, and the agent did. Hillary then ordered the agent to tell the president to "get home now, and I mean right now."

The agent passed the message along to the detail.

"Oh, my God. Clinton loves mingling with

people, and he loves to play golf, but she was having none of that," the agent says. "Clinton was to remain at the Martha's Vineyard estate. He was being punished. It was like he was grounded."

As when they were in the White House, agents say the Clintons argue a lot.

"There seems to be some kind of tension [between them]," one agent says. "There is an uneasiness."

On those rare occasions when Clinton has been photographed kissing his wife, he looks uncomfortable, and she has a look of distaste. Just as Jimmy Carter would carry empty luggage when cameras were around, to try to cover up their chilly relationship, the Clintons make a point of rigidly holding hands in front of photographers.

In contrast to Hillary, since leaving the White House, Bill Clinton is "very friendly to the agents," says one agent. "I think he realizes once he's out of office, we're pretty much all he's got, and he does treat the guys really well."

But as when he was in the White House, Clinton is constantly looking for women, an agent says. "He'll see some attractive women walk by, and you can just see he isn't paying any attention to what anyone is saying. He will actually point out the women. He hasn't changed."

Several years after moving into the Clintons' 5,200-square-foot home in Chappaqua, Bill began seeing the blonde who lives nearby.

"She's a soccer mom type," says an agent, referring to the woman the Secret Service unofficially code-named Energizer. "She's real nice. She brings little snacks for the agents. She is just the opposite of Hillary."

He may be perpetually late, but Bill Clinton times their comings and goings so well that the woman appears almost as soon as Hillary leaves.

"They would miss each other by just minutes," says an agent.

Other agents say their supervisors' instruction to suspend a security check for Energizer and conceal her visits undercuts their mission.

"My problem is with the Secret Service," an agent says. "When you conspire with him to conceal his mistress from his wife, doctor the books, and force your agents to ignore a security plan, you are helping to foster a corrupting culture."

19
DALLAS

If corner cutting has become standard practice in the Secret Service today, it is not without precedent. By definition, an assassination nullifies democracy. Yet despite four assassinations, protection of the president has always been an afterthought.

Even though the Civil War was raging and he received constant threats, Abraham Lincoln refused to agree to the security protection recommended by his aides, friends, and the military. Finally, just before his assassination on April 14, 1865, Lincoln agreed to protection by Washington police officers. Four officers were assigned to the detail. But on the night of Lincoln's assassination at Ford's Theatre, Patrolman John F. Parker decided to wander off to watch the play, then went with Lincoln's footman and coachman for a drink at the nearby Star Saloon.

Parker was an incompetent officer who

had been hauled before the police board numerous times. His infractions included conduct unbecoming an officer, using intemperate language, and being drunk on duty. When brought before the board for frequenting a whorehouse, Parker claimed that the proprietress had sent for him.

As a result of Parker's negligence, as Lincoln watched the play *Our American Cousin,* the president was as unprotected as any private citizen. John Wilkes Booth, a fanatical Confederate sympathizer, made his way to Lincoln's box, snuck in, and shot him in the back of the head. The president died the next morning.

A fellow presidential bodyguard, William H. Crook, held Parker directly responsible for the assassination. "Had he done his duty, I believe President Lincoln would not have been murdered by Booth," Crook wrote in his memoir. "Parker knew that he had failed in duty. He looked like a convicted criminal the next day." Parker should have been fired immediately, but he was not terminated until 1868 — for sleeping on duty.

Despite the tragedy, protection of the president remained haphazard. For a short time after the Civil War, the War Department assigned soldiers to protect the White

House and its grounds. On special occasions, Washington police officers helped maintain order and prevented crowds from assembling. But the permanent detail of four police officers assigned to guard the president during Lincoln's term was reduced to three. These officers protected only the White House and did not receive any special training.

Thus, on the morning of July 2, 1881, when President James A. Garfield walked through a waiting room toward a train in the Baltimore and Potomac Railroad station in Washington on his way to New England, he was as unguarded as Lincoln had been. Emerging from the crowds, Charles J. Guiteau shot the president in the arm and then fatally shot him a second time in the back.

Having delivered a short speech at a small gathering in New York endorsing Garfield's candidacy, Guiteau had come to believe that he had orchestrated Garfield's victory. Guiteau decided he deserved an ambassadorship to Vienna or Paris. When the appointment didn't materialize, Guiteau had a divine revelation that came "like a flash" as he lay in bed: God commanded him to kill the ungrateful president. On September 19, 1881, Garfield died of his wounds. He had been president just four months.

Even then, steps were not taken to protect the next president, Chester A. Arthur. The resistance to doing so was rooted in the perennial question of how to reconcile the need to protect the country's leaders with their need to mingle with citizens and not lose touch with their concerns.

After Garfield's assassination, the *New York Tribune* warned against improving security. The paper said that the country did not want the president to become "the slave of his office, the prisoner of forms and restrictions." Other critics railed about what was called "royalism" — surrounding the president with courtiers and guards, the trappings of the English monarchy.

Given the competing aims, the hit-or-miss way the Secret Service stumbled into protecting the president is not surprising. The agency began operating as a division of the Treasury Department on July 5, 1865, to track down and arrest counterfeiters — not assassins. Back then, an estimated one-third of the nation's currency was counterfeit. States issued their own currency, printed by sixteen hundred state banks. Some seven thousand varieties of these notes were in circulation, each with a different design. Nobody knew what their money was supposed to look like.

Ironically, Abraham Lincoln's last official act on the day he was shot was to sign into law the legislation creating the Secret Service. By 1867, the Secret Service had brought counterfeiting largely under control. With the agency's success, Congress gave it broader authority to investigate other crimes, including fraud against the government. That led circuitously to the Secret Service's mission today.

In 1894, the Secret Service was investigating a plot to assassinate President Grover Cleveland by a group of "western gamblers, anarchists, or cranks" in Colorado. Exceeding its mandate, the agency assigned two men who had been conducting the investigation to protect Cleveland at special events and on trips. The two agents rode in a buggy behind his carriage. But after political opponents criticized him for receiving protection, Cleveland told the agents he did not want their help.

As the number of threatening letters addressed to the president increased, Cleveland's wife persuaded him to beef up protection at the White House. The number of police assigned to guard the White House rose from three to twenty-seven. In 1894, the Secret Service began to supplement that protection by assigning agents to protect the president on an informal basis, including when the president traveled.

Yet that did not help William McKinley, the next president. Three Secret Service agents were with him when Leon F. Czolgosz, a twenty-eight-year-old self-styled anarchist, shot him on September 6, 1901. McKinley was attending a reception that day in the Temple of Music at the Pan American Exposition in Buffalo, New York. Long lines of citizens passed between policemen and soldiers to shake his hand. Czolgosz had waited for more than two hours in eighty-two-degree heat for his turn. He shot the president twice with a pistol concealed in a handkerchief. Bullets slammed into McKinley's chest and stomach. Eight days later, the president died of blood poisoning.

In a handwritten confession, Czolgosz said, "When I shot him [McKinley], I intended to kill him, and the reason for my intention in killing was because I did not believe in presidents over us. I was willing to sacrifice myself & the president for the benefit of the country. I felt I had more courage than the average man in killing [sic] president and was willing to put my own life at stake in order to do it."

Still, legislative reaction was agonizingly slow. It was not until a year later that the Secret Service officially assumed responsibility for protecting the president. Even then it lacked statutory authority to do so. While Congress began allocating funds expressly for the purpose in 1906, it did so annually as part of the Sundry Civil Expenses Act.

Presidents tended to scoff at the dangers they faced. President Theodore Roosevelt wrote to Senator Henry Cabot Lodge that he considered the Secret Service to be a "very small but very necessary thorn in the flesh. Of course," he wrote, "they would not be the least use in preventing any assault upon my life. I do not believe there is any danger of such an assault, and if there were, as Lincoln said, 'Though it would be safer for a president to live in a cage, it would interfere with his business.' "

Unsuccessful assassination attempts were made on President Andrew Jackson on January 30, 1835, President Theodore Roosevelt on October 14, 1912, and Franklin D. Roosevelt on February 15, 1933, before he was sworn in the following month. Yet when it came to protection of the president, Congress continued to drag its feet. Although it kept considering bills to make it a federal crime to assassinate the president,

Congress failed to act. Members of the public continued to be free to roam the White House during daylight hours.

Finally, at the Secret Service's insistence, public access to the White House grounds was banned for the first time during World War II. To enter the White House, visitors had to report to guard posts at gates around the perimeter. By then, Congress had formally established the White House Police in 1922 to guard the complex and secure the grounds. In 1930, that police agency was folded into the Secret Service, and it is now called the Secret Service's Uniformed Division.

By the end of World War II, the number of agents assigned to protect the president had been increased to thirty-seven. That increased security soon paid off. At 2:20 P.M. on November 1, 1950, two Puerto Rican nationalists tried to force their way into Blair House, across the street from the White House, to kill President Harry S. Truman. The president was staying there while the White House was being renovated. Truman — code-named Supervise — was napping on the second floor. As usual, Bess Truman — code-named Sunnyside — was out of town. She hated Washington.

The would-be assassins, Oscar Collazo,

thirty-six, and Griselio Torresola, twenty-five, hoped to draw attention to the cause of separating Puerto Rico from the United States. Agents and White House Police officers took down the gunmen. But White House Police officer Leslie Coffelt died in surgery four hours later. In a last heroic act, Coffelt had leaped to his feet and propped himself against his security booth. He pointed his revolver at Torresola's head and fired. The bullet ripped through Torresola's ear. The would-be assassin pitched forward, dead on the street. Coffelt earned a place on the Secret Service's Honor Roll of personnel killed in the line of duty.

Two other White House policemen and Collazo recovered from their wounds. A total of twenty-seven shots had been fired. The biggest gunfight in Secret Service history lasted a mere forty seconds.

The following year Congress finally passed legislation to permanently authorize the Secret Service to protect the president, his immediate family, the president-elect, and if he requests it, the vice president. In 1962, Congress expanded protection to include the vice president, vice president-elect, and the next officer to succeed the president. Under current law, their immediate families receive protection as well. Since the next officer to succeed the president is the speaker of the House, and he is protected by the Capitol Police, the Secret Service does not protect him.

While they may not decline protection, it is up to those who are by law given Secret Service protection just how much they receive. By their very nature presidents want more exposure, while Secret Service agents want more security, leading to inherent tension. As President Kennedy's aide Kenneth O'Donnell said, "The president's views of his responsibilities as president of the United States were that he meet the people, that he go out to their homes and see them, and allow them to see him, and discuss, if possible, the views of the world as he sees it, the problems of the country as he sees them."

Before his trip to Dallas on November 22, 1963, Kennedy received warnings about potential violence there. United Nations ambassador Adlai Stevenson called Kennedy aide Arthur Schlesinger Jr. and urged him to tell the president not to go. Stevenson had just spoken in Dallas, where he said demonstrators had confronted him, cursing and spitting on him. Senator J. William Fulbright also warned Kennedy.

"Dallas is a very dangerous place," Fulbright told him. "I wouldn't go there. Don't you go."

Just as Vice President Joe Biden is oblivious today to the need for a full escort of agents when traveling in Delaware, Kennedy brushed aside the warnings. Kennedy aide O'Donnell told the Secret Service that unless it was raining, the president wanted to ride in an open convertible, according to the Warren Commission Report, which was largely based on the FBI's exhaustive investigation. If it was raining, Kennedy would use a plastic top that was not bulletproof. Kennedy — code-named Lancer — personally told agents he did not want them to ride on the small running boards at the rear of the car.

Moreover, only two Secret Service agents had traveled to Dallas to make advance preparations for the trip. At the time, the advance protocol did not include an inspection of buildings along the motorcade route, which was publicized in advance. In all, Kennedy's Secret Service detail consisted of about twenty-four agents, or seven agents per shift. Another twelve agents protected Jackie Kennedy and the president's two children.

At 12:30 P.M., the president's limousine was traveling at about eleven miles per hour.

Shots resounded in rapid succession from the Texas Book Depository. A bullet entered the base of the back of the president's neck. Another bullet then struck him in the back of the head, causing a massive, fatal wound. He fell to the left, onto his wife Jackie's lap.

Agent William R. Greer was driving the limo; agent Roy H. Kellerman was sitting to his right. Neither agent could immediately leap to Kennedy's assistance, as would have been the case if agents had been allowed to ride at the rear of the car. Between them and Kennedy was a second row of seats between the front and rear seats, making it more difficult for the agents to protect the president. The "kill shot" to the president's head came at least 4.8 seconds after the first shot that hit him. If they had been there, the interval would have given agents on the rear running board of the limousine plenty of time to jump on the president, push him to the floor, and shield him from the bullet that took his life.

Agent Clinton J. Hill, riding on the left running board of the follow-up car, raced toward Kennedy's limousine. He pulled himself onto the back of the car as it gained speed. He pushed Jackie — code-named Lace — back into the rear seat as he shielded both her and the president.

248

"If agents had been allowed on the rear running boards, they would have pushed the president down and jumped on him to protect him before the fatal shot," Charles "Chuck" Taylor, who was an agent on the Kennedy detail, tells me.

Secret Service director Lewis Merletti later confirmed that. "An analysis of the ensuing assassination — including the trajectory of the bullets which struck the president — indicates that it might have been thwarted had agents been stationed on the car's running boards," Merletti said.

In typical Washington fashion, the Secret Service took corrective measures when it was too late. Following the Kennedy assassination, the agency doubled its complement of agents, computerized and increased its intelligence data, bolstered the number of agents assigned to advance and intelligence work, created countersniper teams, expanded training functions, and improved liaison with other law enforcement and federal agencies.

It was but another tragic example of how undercutting protection can make the president vulnerable to assassination. Now that they can constantly interact with the populace through electronic media, presidents have even less excuse to ignore Secret

Service security advice. By following that advice, presidents can do two things at once: greet the public while sparing the country the agony of another assassination.

20
OPERATION MOONLIGHT

The Marine One helicopter carrying President Obama and his family was preparing to lift off from the South Lawn of the White House when the order came into the Washington field office from Secret Service director Mark Sullivan: Instead of protecting the president by watching for snipers, agents were to speed to southern Maryland to watch over Sullivan's assistant, Lisa L. Chopey, at her home.

The secret assignment, called Operation Moonlight, entailed dispatching two Secret Service agents on two daily eight-hour shifts over at least two months beginning in July 2011 to drive at taxpayer expense to check on the "welfare" of Chopey, forty-one, after she and her father were allegedly harassed by Michael J. Mulligan Sr., her forty-three-year-old neighbor.

As part of the personal favor to Sullivan's assistant, stunned agents were also instructed to retrieve confidential law enforcement and financial records on Mulligan. Sullivan's instruction to supervisors was that agents were not to tell anyone what they were doing, outside of their own thirty-five-agent Protective Intelligence Squad in the Washington field office at 1100 L Street NW.

Copies of Secret Service records kept at the Washington field office confirm the instruction to regularly go to Chopey's home in La Plata, Maryland, "to make sure everything is all right" after the altercation with Mulligan.

Chopey had already reported the altercation to the police, and two officers had responded. The Secret Service has no legal authority to protect its own employees, and criminal law prohibits retrieving confidential information for any reason not related to official law enforcement duties. What's more, as a result of Sullivan's diversion of agents, critical posts for protecting President Obama and Vice President Biden went unmanned.

Agents were told the altercation with Mulligan occurred as Chopey was about to leave for work. Mulligan had had a previous dispute with Chopey's father, Peter Tritola, who lived with her, and Mulligan had allegedly assaulted him. The Secret Service file includes a petition for a restraining order — known locally as a peace order — filed against Mulligan with the District Court of Maryland for Charles County. Signed by Chopey under penalty of perjury, the public document lists her address on Huntt Road in La Plata.

According to her account, Chopey arrived at the entrance to Huntt Road around 7:35 A.M. on June 30, 2011, and stopped to check her mailbox there. She then returned to her vehicle and drove toward her residence. A green all-terrain four-wheeler with Mulligan at the wheel came speeding toward her, circled her vehicle several times, and cut in front of her, forcing her to stop. The driver spun its tires to throw rocks and gravel toward her.

The four-wheeler then began circling Tritola, who had come outside. Mulligan spun its wheels, spewing rocks and gravel at him and at Chopey's brother and niece, who also had come outside upon hearing the commotion. Chopey wrote that she called local police, and two officers arrived at her residence. She obtained a court order barring Mulligan from contacting her, entering the grounds of her home, or harassing her. Mulligan subsequently entered an Alford plea, meaning he admitted the prosecution would likely prove its second degree assault charge against him. He was ultimately sentenced in Circuit Court for Charles County to a suspended jail term of six months and three years of unsupervised probation.

When the instruction to watch over Chopey came in on July 1, "a supervisor called the two agents scheduled to conduct surveillance of Marine One and told them to discontinue their assignment and come to the field office," an agent says. When they arrived on the sixth floor of the field office, they were given Google map directions from the office to Chopey's home and told to drive there and watch out for her. The Google map directions are contained in the Secret Service file, along with a handwritten notation to use a GPS tracking device instead.

"They gave these two agents a brief summary of what had happened and said do a welfare check and make sure this individual is not near them," an agent says. "They're supposed to make sure she's okay and not being harassed by this gentleman. They went out there and were told to make telephonic contact with her each time."

The two agents "are presented with a difficult challenge, because they don't have any authority to do that," the agent says. "This [assignment] has nothing to do with the Secret Service, but to make this even worse, the supervisor tells the guys, 'By the way, you don't discuss this outside the Protective Intelligence Squad. This is a personal favor for the director, and we can't talk about this.' It was at the direction of Director Sullivan, but his name is conveniently missing from the file, which was kept at the supervisor's desk on the sixth floor."

As an agent, "your position does not entitle you to give Lisa Chopey personal protection by the Secret Service," the agent says. "The Congress, not the director, mandates to whom we give protection. You cannot pick and choose who you want to give protection to."

A copy of a U.S. Secret Service Command Post Protectee Log in the file shows that beginning on Friday, July 1, 2011, agents wrote their names and signed their initials with times and dates when they went to check on Chopey and her father. That included when agents were diverted from conducting surveillance as Obama's helicopter lifted off from the South Lawn at 4:30 P.M. on July 1. The helicopter was transporting President Obama, Michelle

Obama, and their two daughters to Camp David for the weekend.

The Secret Service file contains copies of law enforcement and financial records that agents retrieved, including any arrest records, as part of a background investigation of Mulligan. Given that it was a clandestine assignment outside the lawful authority of the Secret Service, the file was kept separate from the agency's official records. Instead, it was hidden on a lower shelf of the supervisor's platform in the operations center on the sixth floor of the Washington field office.

Unlike the FBI, the Secret Service does not label its cases with names like ABSCAM or UNABOM. But Secret Service agents in the Washington field office were told the clandestine mission to protect Chopey and her father would be unofficially referred to as Operation Moonlight.

While the file makes no mention of Sullivan, an agent says the orders came from him through supervisors in the field office. Agents would not have responded to such an alarming order on behalf of Sullivan's assistant unless it had come from the director himself, an agent notes.

"Sullivan directed agents in the Washington field office to conduct a full background check of this guy when it had nothing to do with the Secret Service," an agent says. "It's illegal. You can't run NCIC [National Crime Information Center], LexisNexis Accurint for Law Enforcement, and discover all of this individual's financial records, background records, and criminal histories when it doesn't involve the agency for which you work."

Moreover, "agents in the Protective Intelligence Squad knew what they were doing was wrong, and management knew it was wrong," the agent says. "The agents knew on a daily basis they were doing something that did not involve the Secret Service with taxpayer dollars. They were told not to discuss this outside the squad, that they were going to take care of this themselves on the direction of the director."

The agents diverted to check on Chopey were on a team code-named Prowler. Consisting of two agents per shift, Prowler conducts covert surveillance to detect any threats when Marine One lifts off or lands with the president and when Marine Two lifts off or lands with the vice president. Armed with Remington breaching shotguns and Heckler & Koch MP5 submachine guns, as well as their handguns, the agents typically conduct surveillance from an unmarked truck outside the White House or at the vice president's residence at the Naval Observatory.

Agents assigned to Prowler were told to leave their posts, drive to Chopey's home, and sit outside. Depending on traffic, the trip takes one to two hours. If Chopey was at work, they were instructed to call her on her cell phone to ask where she was and then watch over her father until it was time for them to drive back to Washington to end their shifts. If they had any questions, they were to call a high-level supervisor listed in the file.

Requiring agents to sign their initials to verify that they have gone to a post is highly unusual. "We protect the president and his wife and daughters and do not have to initial that we have performed our duties," an agent says.

After five days, the agents stopped signing the log because they recognized that since their activity was unlawful, the document could be used as evidence against them, according to a current agent.

When Prowler agents were occupied watching Chopey's house, no other agents were assigned to perform their duties. That left an open door to a potential attack on the president: A sniper or a Stinger missile launched from the perimeter of the White House grounds could have downed Marine One. In fact, the Secret Service had previously received intelligence that a terrorist organization was considering such an attack. Yet an agent says that this possibility seemed not to concern Secret Service management.

The Prowler team was also diverted from the other duties assigned to it. They include covering the motorcades of the president and vice president as they enter and leave the White House grounds, checking for suspicious persons around the White House, and following up on and investigating threats to the president or vice president. If an attack had occurred, the team would not have been there to help repel it.

"If you had to cover the president or the vice president, that was secondary," an agent says. "It was to check on her house. We don't have any authority in Maryland. If something happened, we couldn't do anything anyway."

The Secret Service file shows that as instructed, on July 1, Secret Service agents conducted a complete background investigation of Mulligan that included retrieving confidential information from the FBI's National Crime Information Center

(NCIC) and LexisNexis Accurint for Law Enforcement. Printouts of the responses in the Secret Service file are dated the same day.

The retrieved reports plainly show that the Secret Service requested them, and two of the reports list the name of the Secret Service agent who ordered the records. They show Mulligan's Social Security number, date of birth, prior residences, photos of him, personal details of his life, and any arrest records.

The Secret Service file also includes an agency employee printout on Chopey. It shows a photo of the attractive woman, her cell phone number, her GS-13 federal salary level, and the fact that her position was staff assistant in the Office of the Director. She began working for the Secret Service in June 1993.

Federal law makes it a crime to threaten or retaliate against a federal law enforcement officer while he or she is performing official duties. But beyond this limited set of circumstances, neither the Secret Service nor the FBI has authority to respond if a support employee such as Chopey, who is not a law enforcement officer and was not performing official duties, encounters a problem requiring police assistance.

Law enforcement officers are periodically fired and prosecuted for obtaining confidential records for their personal use or for misusing agency resources. In 2008, FBI supervisory agent Mark Rossini pleaded guilty to searching FBI records on behalf of his girlfriend. In 1993, President Clinton dismissed FBI director William S. Sessions over his use of the FBI for enhancements to his home and other personal abuses disclosed in my book *The FBI: Inside the World's Most Powerful Law Enforcement Agency.*

"Mark Sullivan has come up through the career ranks," says John L. Martin, who headed the Justice Department's counterespionage section for nearly twenty-five years and supervised the prosecution of seventy-six spies. "He of all people should know better than to misuse his official position for personal reasons. That is a crime, as is obtaining law enforcement or financial information for personal reasons." Martin says it is now up to the FBI to launch a criminal investigation.

Asked for comment, Secret Service spokesman Edwin Donovan said that as a result of an assault on Lisa Chopey's father and the subsequent harassment of Chopey herself, a "Washington field office patrol vehicle, which is assigned to the Washington field office, made a handful of checks over the following weekend." Donovan added, "Any suggestion that assets were drawn away from other assignments or that it lasted more than several days is false." He said, "This was not a 'secret' operation as described by these unnamed sources, but a rather mundane security check that many employees were aware of as it was ongoing."

After being given a copy of the Secret Service file, Donovan did not cite any legal authority that would give the Secret Service the right to provide protection to its own employees or to check the criminal backgrounds of anyone who may have harassed them. Nor, when asked for comment, did Donovan deny that Sullivan ordered the mission or that he violated criminal laws in doing so. Instead, Donovan said, "The Secret Service conducts hundreds of thousands of NCIC checks each year and is regularly audited by the Criminal Justice Information Service Advisory Policy Board."

Sullivan, who resigned as director in February 2013, did not respond to a voice mail in October 2012 seeking comment. Chopey declined to comment.

In May 2014, the *Washington Post* ran a story disclosing the existence of Operation Moonlight, but the story was not based on access to the Secret Service file and lacked many of the most important details of the operation, including the fact that agents illegally retrieved confidential law-enforcement records on Mulligan.

A spokesman for Sullivan told the *Post* that the director had had nothing to do with ordering protection for his own assistant. Instead, Sullivan said a supervisor in his office authorized the operation, that he did not learn about it until after it had begun, and that the checks were conducted for only a few days and were "appropriate." Mulligan told the paper Chopey tried to hurt him with her SUV when he was trying to talk with her about tensions between the families. He said imposing-looking vehicles parked near Chopey's home for "months."

The fact that a man who was director of the Secret Service for seven years could maintain that diverting agents from watching for snipers as President Obama and his family lifted off in Marine One to instead protecting his own assistant at her home was "appropriate" spotlights the supreme arrogance of Secret Service management.

The Secret Service agents involved in

Operation Moonlight were fully aware that they were breaking the law, but they felt that their jobs were on the line, an agent says. The agents "obtained all this information illegally and kept it and were told not to talk about it outside the squad," an agent says. "They kept records at the duty desk and made agents on every shift initial that they had gone all the way out to southern Maryland to check on the woman's welfare on the tax-payer dollar."

The revelation of this abuse of power is consistent with practices exposed in this book: Secret Service management dishonestly instructing agents to fill out their own physical fitness test scores, rigging law enforcement scenarios presented to members of Congress, padding arrest statistics, ordering agents to ignore basic security procedures such as passing people through magnetometers at events, and instructing agents to let Bradley Cooper's unscreened vehicle into a secure area where Obama was about to speak.

Sullivan's order was a "direct example of the Secret Service management mind-set, showing disregard for how serious our job really is," an agent says. "Because of a personal agenda to do a personal favor, the director used tax dollars, illegally violated a man's personal privacy, and endangered the president of the United States."

21
MISSING SUNGLASSES

Secret Service agents found George W. Bush to be respectful and considerate of them, and few protectees were as loved by agents as Laura Bush. Agents were overjoyed at the contrast with their predecessors, the Clintons. But especially when they were younger, the Bushes' twin daughters, Jenna and Barbara, gave agents fits.

"With Bush, there was an instant change," a former Secret Service agent says. "He was punctual. Clinton was never on time for anything. It was embarrassing. Bush and his wife treated you normally, decently. They had conversations with us. The Clintons were arrogant, standoffish, and paranoid. Everyone got a morale boost with Bush. He was the complete opposite of Clinton."

"Bush is down-to-earth, caring," another agent says. The Bushes offer food to agents. "They are always thinking of people around them." Compared with the Clintons, the difference "is striking."

Under Clinton, the White House operated like an all-night pizza parlor. Aides attended meetings in jeans and T-shirts. As in a college debating society, business was conducted late into the night and all weekend. Clinton threw out ideas and endlessly circled a subject rather than come to a conclusion. He did not hesitate to wake up aides at home with trivial questions. The lobby of the West Wing was like a subway station, packed with visitors coming and going. Carpets and upholstered furniture were fraying, and empty pizza containers were everywhere.

"Under Clinton, staffers would bring in girls they had picked up in Georgetown to see the Oval Office at midnight," says a former Secret Service agent. "[George W.] Bush changed that. If a staffer wanted to bring a guest in, he had to make an appointment in advance. There were no more late-night visits to the Oval Office. Bush restored respect."

In contrast to first daughter Chelsea Clinton, Jenna and Barbara Bush thought of Secret Service protection as a pain and treated agents as if they were the enemy. When she was attending the University of Texas, Jenna decided to sleep over at a friend's home in Highland Park, four miles north of downtown Dallas. All night, agents watched over the house, thinking Jenna was there. The next morning, Jenna — code-named Twinkle — told one of the agents that during the previous evening, she had left her sunglasses at Texadelphia, a nearby cheese steak hangout. She said she wanted to try to retrieve them.

The agent offered to pick them up himself, and he located them at the restaurant. But it was clear that the president's daughter had bamboozled the detail once again, eluding her agents as they were watching over her friend's house during the night.

"Jenna snuck out of the house to go to the restaurant," the former agent says. "Instead of letting us know where and when she was going, she would just run out and jump in her car and go. It got to the point where instead of staying at a location inside and then preparing the vehicles, agents had to pretty much stay posted up in the cars all day because she wouldn't provide notice and would just run out."

Even though the agents dressed in casual clothes like shorts and jeans, and most people were unaware of their role, both girls resented having Secret Service agents around. Jenna would purposely try to lose her protection by running red lights or by jumping in her car without telling agents where she was going. As a result, the Secret Service had to keep her car under surveillance at the White House so agents could follow her — a complete waste of manpower. Similarly, when Barbara was attending Yale, she would sneak out of her dormitory, eluding her agents.

"These girls didn't want protection," says a former agent who was on their details. "They would try to run from us and hide from us. They'd intentionally try to lose us, wouldn't tell us where they were going. They'd hop in a car and take off, not notify the detail they were leaving."

"The supervisor of her [Jenna's] detail was scared of her, because they were afraid that she was going to pick up the phone and call Dad," an agent says.

In fact, Jenna called her father many times when she wanted the agents to back off. "The president would call the special agent in charge," the agent says. "The SAIC would call the detail leader, the detail leader would call the guys and say, 'Hey, you've got to back off.'"

"How about us doing our jobs?" an agent said when he was still protecting her. "I mean what if something happens to her? I think she has a hard time grasping how easy it would be to pick her up, throw her in a van, and next thing you know she's on Al Jazeera. And we're out there, we're trying to do the right thing. And I don't think she understands it. She definitely didn't respect what we're out there trying to do for her."

"When they were out in California, Jenna and Barbara went skydiving," a former agent says. "I remember that the first lady called up the detail leader and reamed him out because we had let them go skydiving. But we can't tell them no, you can't go skydiving, Mommy and Daddy say no."

When agents tried to tell Jenna she could not do something, "she was like, 'Well, I'm going to do it,' and the first thing she does is pick up the phone and call Daddy. Then you got to call your boss and say, 'Listen, she just had a conversation with POTUS,' and it gets all spun up the chain of command."

While Bush was being shortsighted in siding with his daughter over the Secret Service, agents often tend to go along with whatever the president wants without explaining the possible dire security consequences.

To make matters worse, President Bush would occasionally chew out the detail for *not* following his daughter. One afternoon at the White House, Jenna snuck out a back exit that leads to the Rose Garden, dodging her detail. Bush saw her leave and called the detail leader to complain that she was not being followed.

"She stepped up to the plate and said, 'Daddy, I didn't tell them where I was going,' " an agent says.

One detail leader found he could give Jenna instructions, and she would listen.

"He could call her up on the phone and be like, 'Jenna, what the hell are you doing?' They were buddies. They were pals. He was strictly professional, but he knew how to deal with her. He could tell her, 'Listen, Jenna, you're killing me. You gotta tell me what's going on.' And she respected him, which was great."

Still, says another agent, "every day we'd run the risk of losing her. She never told us where she was going. It was rare. Sometimes she'd tell Neil [the detail leader], and Neil would get the scoop of what was going on, and Neil would try hard to get that information."

Agents say Jenna's twin, Barbara — code-named Turquoise — was almost as difficult as Jenna. When Barbara was attending Yale, she would jump in her car with friends and drive to New York, where she would stay overnight, never giving her agents advance warning.

"Agents learned to pack a bag with clothing, because it became a habit for both Barbara and Jenna to say, 'I want to go to the airport, I want to fly to New York,' " an agent says. "These guys were prepared to work an evening shift, and all of a sudden they're going with just the clothes on their backs."

"One night Barbara just hopped in a car and took off to a bar," a former agent says. "Didn't tell the detail, but the counter-surveillance units picked her up the best they could and tried to follow her."

Explaining his own thinking, an agent who was on Jenna's detail says, "Instead of calling somebody to complain about us, just tell us what you're going to do and we'll make it work. But just work with us, instead of trying to play games with us, making our lives miserable."

Determining how to deal with first kids' questionable behavior is always a challenge. As law enforcement officers, Secret Service agents are obligated to make arrests if they see a crime being committed. But if a protectee engages in a minor offense, agents will either look the other way or simply tell the individual to stop.

One afternoon, Jenna and some friends were drinking spiked Cokes in the back of an agent's Suburban on the way to a football game in Texas.

"If they're doing something that could endanger their safety, like excessive drinking, I would step in," the agent who was driving them says. "I wouldn't personally say normal drinking or using marijuana is going to affect their immediate health. We're not there in a law enforcement role. Our job is strictly to protect them. So even though a driver could get a ticket for driving with an open container of alcohol, you just kind of look the other way because I was not drinking, and I know as an agent I'm not going to get a ticket for having an open can in the car. But if they were doing lines of cocaine or something like that, that'd be different because people have died from that kind of thing."

If a protectee began smoking marijuana in his presence, a current agent says, "I would tell the kid to put it out. I'd handle it personally right there."

Back when George McGovern was running for president, Agent Richard Repasky picked up his daughter Teresa McGovern at the Columbus, Ohio, airport. "She gets in the Secret Service car and is in the back and she lights up a joint," Repasky recalls. "The car was reeking of marijuana. What was I going to do, arrest her?"

The 1972 Democratic nominee later wrote a book in which he recounted how Teresa began drinking at age thirteen and was hospitalized for depression after her arrest for smoking pot at age nineteen. While she overcame the problem for a while in her thirties, she returned to drinking and was found frozen to death at age forty-five in a parking lot in Madison, Wisconsin, on the night of December 12, 1994, after a drinking binge.

In a similar vein, long before she announced it publicly in 1989, agents found that Kitty Dukakis, the wife of former Massachusetts governor Michael Dukakis, who ran against George H. W. Bush in the 1988 election, had a drinking problem.

"I would be there at their home in the middle of the night, and she'd come down and get into the cupboards and get some alcohol out of there and drink that," a former agent says.

In her book *Shock,* which came out in 2006, Kitty Dukakis described how she finally overcame a lifetime of depression and battles with drug and alcohol addiction with electroconvulsive therapy.

Agents protecting first children have encountered another special problem. After Walter F. Mondale was nominated to be Carter's vice president, agents set up a watch post in the basement of his Washington home. An agent on Mondale's detail strolled into the watch post and found Mondale's daughter, Eleanor, sitting on the lap of another agent on a swivel office chair. Then sixteen, she was wearing short shorts and apparently had been making out with the agent.

"They were startled and looked embarrassed," the former agent says. "They looked like a couple of teenagers making out. It was shocking."

In a 1998 *Time* magazine profile of her, Eleanor Mondale was described as having fantasized with her best friend about Secret Service agents. She would compile secret lists of "which were mine, and which were hers."

"Eleanor would find out whether an agent was single or not and try to get friendly," former agent Dennis Chomicki says. "She dressed in shorts and tight tops. The agents were like, 'Whoa man, I don't want to get involved in this.' "

A leggy blonde, Eleanor became an actress, television host, and radio personality. She died of cancer in 2011 at the age of fifty-one. Prior to her death, her lawyer said allegations that she had compiled such lists or sat on an agent's lap were "false."

At times, agents wind up acting as emergency medical technicians, as when Henry Hager, whom Jenna later married, became so drunk attending a Halloween party with her that agents took him to Georgetown University Hospital.

Over time, the Bush twins became more mature and demonstrated that they appreciated their detail.

"Around Fourth of July, Jenna had a whole bunch of steaks delivered to our command post," an agent says. "Around Christmas, she gave us all another order of steaks and hot dogs and stuff like that. It's got to be tough being the kid of a president. I can't imagine it."

Even a visit by the president to a longtime friend can be a daunting experience for the friend. When George W. Bush was president, he and Laura had dinner at the home of Clay Johnson III, a close friend from high school whom Bush had named deputy director of the Office of Management and Budget, and his wife, Anne. Guests that evening included Bush's Yale friend Roland W. Betts, one of two principals in Chelsea Piers in New York, and FBI director Robert S. Mueller III and his wife, Ann. Checking out the Johnsons' Spring Valley home in Washington, the Secret Service set up a command post in the basement.

"They asked that drapes be put up in the dining room and suggested a chair in which the president should be seated," Anne Johnson recalls. "Agents were posted around the yard, and no-parking cones were put up in front of the house."

The Secret Service asked the Johnsons to clear a closet big enough to hold at least two people.

"In case of an emergency, an agent was going to grab the president, and the two of them were going to dive in," Anne Johnson says. "That would have been an interesting dive, because GWB would have had Laura by the hair, at the very least."

Archly, Anne Johnson asked an agent, "What should everyone else do in case of an emergency?"

"I only have one client, the president," the agent drily replied.

Agents were always amazed at the difference between Bush in person and the way he came across at press conferences.

"He does not look comfortable in front of

a microphone," an agent who was on his detail says. "With us, he doesn't talk like that, doesn't sound like that. He's funny as hell. Incredible sense of humor, and he'll joke around. He's two different personalities."

"When he had a conversation with his staff, Bush was very thoughtful and very intelligent and spoke very well," says a former agent on his detail. "The problem was that you get a lot of handlers who keep telling you what to say in speeches. I always wish that the American people knew the real George Bush."

Since federal law provides for protection of the children of former presidents only when they are under sixteen, the Secret Service no longer protects Jenna and Barbara. As a rule, former presidents receive few threats. But because of the number of threats still directed at Bush, his detail today consists of seventy-five agents, including agents who protect Laura. While the numbers vary, that is more than the number assigned to other former presidents.

"They want protection for the convenience," a former agent says of former presidents and first ladies. "We do their travel arrangements, we make it possible for them to catch trains and planes, we are their fleet of cars. We allow them to do things the ordinary citizen never could do."

If agents think highly of Bush, it is nothing compared to their feelings about his wife. An agent who was assigned to the Bushes one Christmas remembers how caring Laura — code-named Tempo — was. She talked to him for thirty minutes and seemed apologetic about having to take him away from his family during Christmas.

In contrast to Hillary Clinton, "Laura has the undying admiration of almost every agent," an agent says. "I've never ever heard a negative thing about Laura Bush. Nothing. Everybody loves her to death and respects the hell out of her."

22
WATCH THE HANDS

To most Americans, Secret Service agents are anonymous figures wearing sunglasses, a communications earpiece, and a grim expression. Behind the sunglasses, agents are tuning into a sort of different dimension, looking for any sign of suspicious activity.

Agents focus first on people's hands. They are looking for signs of danger — people who don't seem to fit in, have their hands in their pockets, are sweating or look nervous, or appear as if they have mental problems. Agents lock in on movements, objects, and situations that are out of place.

"We look for a guy wearing an overcoat on a warm day," says former agent William Albracht. "A guy not wearing an overcoat on a cold day. A guy with hands in his pockets. A guy carrying a bag. Anybody that is overenthusiastic, or not enthusiastic. Anybody that stands out, or is constantly looking around. You're looking at the eyes and most importantly the hands. Because where those hands go is the key."

If an agent sees a bystander at a rope line with his hands in his pockets, the agent will say, "Sir, take your hands out of your pockets, take your hands out of your pockets *now.*"

"If he doesn't, you literally reach out and grab the individual's hands and hold them there," Albracht says. "You have agents in the crowd who will then see you're having problems. They'll come up to the crowd, and they'll grab the guy and toss him. They will take him out of there, frisk him, pat him down, and see what his problem is. You are allowed to do that in exigent circumstances in protection because it's so immediate. You don't have time to say, 'Hey, would you mind removing your hands?' I mean if this guy's got a weapon, you need to know right then."

An agent who sees a weapon calls out to fellow agents: "Gun! Gun!"

When on protection duty, Secret Service agents wear the trademark radio earpieces tuned to one of the encrypted channels the service uses. Known as a surveillance kit, the device includes a radio transmitter and receiver that agents keep in their pockets.

Sunglasses are not required, but most agents choose to wear them not only to block the sun but to hide their eyes from onlookers.

"With sunglasses, I can look around and look at you and stare at you, and you don't know if I'm staring at you or not," an agent explains.

To identify themselves at events to other agents and to police, Secret Service agents wear on their left lapels color-coded pins featuring the Secret Service five-pointed star. The pins come in four colors. Each week, agents wear a different color. On the back of the pin is a four-digit number. If the pin is stolen, the number can be entered in the FBI's National Crime Information Center (NCIC). If the pin is found, police return it to the Secret Service.

Pins called hard pins are used to identify White House aides to Secret Service agents. Embossed with the presidential or vice presidential seal, the pins signify that the staffer is entitled to have access to the president or vice president. Wearing the pins, staffers are not required to identify themselves to agents. But Secret Service agents have found that some of Vice President Joe Biden's staffers refuse to wear their pin and huffily demand to be recognized regardless.

On one trip, an agent spotted a Biden staffer not wearing her pin and reminded her to wear it at all times. She agreed to do so, but the next day she was again not wearing her pin. When questioned, she admitted that she had left the pin in her hotel room. This time, even though he recognized her, the agent told her she would not be allowed to walk around freely because she wasn't wearing her pin.

"That's a major operational security violation, to leave your pin in your hotel room," the agent says. "Where a maid has access, where hotel staff has access, where anyone with a key card has access, they could enter your room and take it."

At another event for Biden, an agent refused to let an on-site support staffer go backstage because he was wearing what is called a soft pin, which is color-coded and has no seal. The soft pin allows access only when a visitor is escorted by White House staff wearing a hard pin. When the agent refused to let him roam freely, the man complained to a Biden staffer. The staffer told the agent she didn't have time to escort the man and demanded the agent give him access. When the agent refused to budge, she complained to a high-ranking Secret

Service official.

"Of course, the official said to give everyone access behind the stage without hard pin staff escorts," the agent says. "What we have is complacent senior management who are waiting for their next job in the private sector."

While agents wearing earpieces are easily spotted, Secret Service agents wearing plain clothes and no radio earpieces also circulate within crowds at public events and patrol around the White House. If they spot a problem or vulnerability, they use a cell phone to notify the Joint Ops Center at Secret Service headquarters.

"They're the guys in the crowd," an agent says. "You wouldn't know they were there. They're on the outside looking in during an event and during an advance."

These agents try to think like assassins: How can they breach security?

"It's their job to take apart our plan prior to game day," the agent says. "It's their job to basically say, here are the holes, here are your vulnerabilities, tell us how you're going to plug these holes."

Technicians photograph crowds at presidential events. The images are compared with photos taken at other events — sometimes using facial recognition software — to see if a particular onlooker keeps showing up. If one does, agents look for the individual at future events and investigate further.

Since the attempts on President Ford's life, presidents have generally worn bulletproof vests at public events. They are Kevlar Type Three vests that will stop rounds from most handguns and rifles but not from more powerful weapons. Agents on the president's and vice president's details may wear them at public events, but many agents prefer not to. They are uncomfortable and can make life unbearable on a hot day.

Explaining why he always wears the vests, one agent says, "What good am I if I don't have a vest on if I'm trying to stop a bullet from hitting the president or vice president? I get up and put that vest on every day when I go to work because I think if I can't stop a round, what good am I for this man?"

In developing criminal profiling, FBI agents under the direction of Dr. Roger Depue interviewed assassins and would-be assassins in prison. The subjects included Sirhan B. Sirhan, who killed Bobby Kennedy, and Sara Jane Moore and Lynette "Squeaky" Fromme, both of whom tried to kill President Ford.

The FBI profilers found that assassins generally are unstable individuals looking for attention and notoriety. Assassins often keep diaries. It enhances the importance of their acts. Like most celebrity stalkers, assassins tend to be paranoid and to lack trust in other people.

"Usually loners, they are not relaxed in the presence of others and not practiced or skilled in social interaction," John Douglas, one of the FBI profilers who did the interviews, wrote in his book *Obsessions*. Before an assassination attempt, the perpetrator fantasizes that "this one big event will prove once and for all that he has worth, that he can do and be something. It provides an identity and purpose," Douglas said.

Thus, John Hinckley was convinced that actress Jodie Foster would respect him more if he killed Ronald Reagan. He called his attempt to assassinate Reagan "an act of love."

"Jodie Foster may continue to outwardly ignore me for the rest of her life, but I have made an impression on that young lady that will never fade from her mind," Hinckley wrote to a *New York Times* reporter after being found not guilty by reason of insanity. "I am with Jodie spiritually every day and every night. I have made her one of the most famous actresses in the world. Everybody but everybody knows about John and Jodie. We are a historical couple whether Jodie likes it or not. 'I Am Napoleon.' "

"You have to be hypervigilant," says former agent Jerry Parr, who headed President Reagan's detail when he was shot. Citing the assassinations or attempted assassinations of Reagan, John F. Kennedy, Robert F. Kennedy, Governor George Wallace, Gerald Ford, and Martin Luther King, Parr says, "You know it's out there. You just don't know where."

23
THROWING A FIT

As with President Reagan, agents say they could set their watches by Dick Cheney's schedule.

"If Cheney said he was giving a tour of the vice president's residence at 11:30 A.M., he was there at 11:30 A.M.," former agent Dennis Chomicki says. "Cheney is a very quiet guy in a car. It doesn't mean he's not friendly or he dislikes you. But Cheney's a real businessman, everything was pretty serious and straight up. There weren't too many occasions for jokes, and he was a very likeable protectee."

In contrast to his successor, Joe Biden, with Cheney there was "never an afternoon when you showed up at the White House and were told we're going to Delaware tonight," a Secret Service agent who was on Cheney's detail recalls. "Every agent wanted to go to the Cheney detail because he cared about agents' quality of life."

"Dick Cheney was one of the best protectees we've ever had," a current agent says. "He never ever questioned security. He never ever questioned how we did things or why we did things. He knew and respected what we had to do as the Secret Service. That man's schedule was projected out a year at a time."

As a result, "you knew that you were going to be in Washington for these months, and he went to Jackson Hole for the summer, and he went to the Eastern Shore every other weekend or every third weekend," the agent says. "But you knew far in advance when you were going to be out of town."

A gourmet cook, Cheney loved to shop for himself at the Gourmet Giant grocery store in McLean, Virginia.

"We'd just let him go in the store and run around, and we'd try to keep as low a profile as we could," Chomicki says. "Then he'd come out with all his groceries, he'd throw them in the car, and we'd take off. His grandfather was a chef on the Union Pacific Railroad, and he used to take VP Cheney with him on a train, and he taught him how to cook."

The Cheneys would invite agents and their families to the Christmas party they gave every year and stood for photos with them.

"I remember that I was probably the one hundred sixtieth click that afternoon, but when my kids walked up, Mrs. Cheney acted like we were the first picture of the day," an agent who was on the vice president's detail says. "She squatted down and reached out and hugged my little girl, and it really meant a lot to me."

While federal law authorizes the Secret Service to protect the president, president-elect, vice president, and vice president-elect, and their immediate families, the president may extend protection to others, such as top White House aides and the grandchildren of the president or vice president. In the case of Cheney, protection was provided to his two daughters and grandchildren. Including Dick Cheney, that meant nine people got protection. Today Vice President Joe Biden's five grandchildren are also protected.

When President Bush extended protection to the Cheney grandchildren, the Secret Service did not add additional agents. Instead, the agency made do by extending hours and paying overtime to agents on the VP's detail and by borrowing agents from field offices. That allowed no time for the required refresher training, physical fitness tests, and firearms practice.

"Instead of saying, 'Well, we'll be glad to take care of his grandkids, but let's just do the right thing and get some more people over here so we can cover all these added assignments,' Secret Service management said to the president, 'No problem, sir, we'll take care of it,' without giving us any more people," says an agent who was on the vice president's detail.

"You end up working twelve-hour days sitting in a cul-de-sac," says another agent on the detail. "That's why you don't get the training, because you're having to fill in these assignments. You're fighting battles on a multitude of fronts, because you've got the protectees you're trying to make happy, and you turn around and see people we work for who don't care about us at all. It leaves you with feelings of hopelessness, and that's why people want to leave."

While Cheney's daughter Liz treated agents properly when her father was vice president, his daughter Mary was difficult and demanding. Before Mary — code-named Alpine — had a child, the Secret Service provided full protection only to her older sister, Liz, since she had kids. Mary had partial protection: Agents drove her to and from work. But according to agents, Mary seemed to feel competitive.

"She got all up in arms because we sat outside her sister's house all night long. She said, 'Well I think I should have that, too,' " an agent says.

Mary also whined about the Secret Service vehicle assigned to her.

"She saw that her sister had a brand-new Suburban," an agent who was on her detail says. "Mary had an older vehicle. She was like, 'Why can't I have one?' Next thing you know, within a day or two, she has a brand-new Suburban from the Secret Service sitting out there in front of her house."

When her Suburban sustained some damage, the Secret Service chauffeured her in the older vehicle until the new one could be repaired.

"When she saw her old vehicle was brought back to use as her limo, she threw a fit," an agent says. "She called bosses demanding her Suburban be brought back immediately, not realizing that it takes time to make repairs."

Mary also objected to agents standing post overnight at the back of her home. They disturbed her dogs, she said.

"I don't even know what the back side of her house looks like because she won't let us walk around the back because of the dogs," an agent observed when he was on her detail. "Her dogs start barking. It gets them all upset if we go back there. So we've got some cameras angled back there. But your hands are tied. It's a thankless job anyway, but then you've got protectees who mandate how you're going to do your job."

When an agent on Mary Cheney's detail went on vacation, another agent filled in on a temporary basis. Not being aware of what exit she would take, he missed her departure from her office in Washington.

"She shot an e-mail to a supervisor in our operations section saying that you need to stop putting temps on my shift, I'm getting sick of it, I'm tired of being a tour guide around here," an agent who was on her detail says. If it happened again, she said, she was going to complain to the special agent in charge of the vice president's detail.

When Mary demanded that the Secret Service shuttle her friends out to restaurants, her detail leader refused, as he should have. Secret Service agents are law enforcement officers, not taxi drivers, and they are authorized to protect only specific individuals. But Mary threw a fit and got Secret Service management to remove the leader from her detail. That sent a message to all agents: You do your job and follow the rules, and management may not back you.

Asked for comment, Mary Cheney said, "These stories are simply not true, and I have nothing but the utmost respect for the men and women of the Secret Service. I am deeply appreciative of everything they have done to keep my family safe."

While protecting Dick Cheney, agents were told that a specific, credible threat had been picked up regarding his grandchildren. Normally, one agent was assigned to each grandchild. As a result of the threat information, "agents carrying MP5s doubled up and quadrupled up in cars behind these kids when they were going to the mall and the movies," an agent says.

Even though they were known, Secret Service management did not share any details of the threat. The agents had no idea who or what to look out for. Only later did they learn that the threat came from intercepted communications of terrorists in the Middle East.

"Secret Service senior management in this particular case guarded its own information and prevented the working agents from getting the intelligence they needed to get the job done," an agent says. "This is my life you're talking about. If it's a specific, credible threat against us, against them, that includes me. At least I'll know what I'm looking for if it comes my way."

Dick Cheney had the Secret Service code name Angler, while Lynne Cheney was Author. When assigning code names to protectees, the Secret Service starts with a random list of words, all beginning with the same letter for each family. The code names were once necessary because Secret Service radio transmissions were not encrypted. Now that they are, the Secret Service continues to use code names to avoid confusion when pronouncing the names of protectees. In addition, by using code names, agents prevent people who may overhear a live conversation from recognizing the subject of the conversation.

Produced by the White House Communications Agency, the list of code names excludes words that are offensive or may be easily mistaken for other words. However, those under protection may object to a code name and propose another. Thus, Lynne Cheney, a prolific author, asked for and was given the Secret Service code name Author. Dick Cheney, an avid fisherman, got the code name Angler.

George W. Bush objected to Tumbler, the code name he was initially assigned. Perhaps it reminded him of his drinking days. Instead, he chose Trailblazer. Bush's chief of staff Josh Bolton chose Fatboy, referring to the Fat Boy model of his silver-and-black Harley-Davidson. His predecessor, Andy Card, was Patriot, a code name the Secret Service chose when Card said he did not like his assigned name Potomac.

With two exceptions, agents had no problems with the rest of the Bush administration. The exceptions were Treasury Secretary John Snow and Homeland Security Secretary Tom Ridge. Ridge was incredibly cheap. On weekends, he would return to his home in Erie, Pennsylvania, and so that he would not have to pay for his own plane ticket, he would insist that agents drive him. The trip from Washington was more than six hours.

"The guy would make them motorcade to Erie, Pennsylvania, almost every other weekend, or every weekend, because he didn't want to pay for a plane ticket," an agent who was on his detail says. "If the guy found a free meal, he was there. His reputation in the service was he was the biggest cheapskate ever."

Instead of buying a newspaper at hotels, Ridge would ask agents for their copy of the paper.

"If somebody said, 'Hey, Mr. Secretary, appreciate it, meal's on us,' Ridge would go back there the next night to the same restaurant and see how long he could milk a free meal from this place," an agent says.

Agents liked John Snow because he loved to chat and joke with them.

"John Snow was kind of a pretty cool protectee, in that he knew every guy on the detail," an agent says. "He'd sit in the back of his limo, and he'd talk with you. It was like a group of guys hanging out."

But Snow, a former chairman and chief executive officer of CSX Corporation, had what agents on his detail believed was a mistress in Richmond, where he and his wife had lived. While Snow rented and later bought an apartment in Washington, he would travel back to his hometown almost every weekend. That incurred huge expenses for taxpayers because agents had to drive him the two hours to Richmond and stay in hotels there.

The Secret Service gave the woman the unofficial code name Area 51, after the supersecret Air Force testing ground in Nevada that gives rise to conspiracy theories.

Now chairman of Cerberus Capital Management, Snow commented through his

Richmond lawyer Richard Cullen, a former Virginia state attorney general and personal friend of the Snows for more than twenty-five years.

"John Snow did not have an affair," Cullen said. "The agents who refuse to identify themselves in making this accusation are simply and sadly very wrong."

But agents who were on Snow's detail say otherwise. Snow "was messing around quite a bit, and it was pretty disturbing to the guys on the detail, because we knew we were away from home for the express purpose of him to meet up with his mistress," says a former agent who was on his detail.

One morning, an agent was walking by the front window of Snow's house in Richmond and saw Snow and the alleged mistress kissing. At another point, the woman's husband came home while Snow was seeing her in the couple's home. An agent banged the doors of his Suburban and called out the husband's name to try to alert Snow. As the husband was walking into his house, Snow came out, his hair messed up.

The woman would also fly to Washington and see Snow at his rented apartment.

"She knew all of us by name," a former agent says. "She'd just come out of the woodwork out of nowhere and say, 'Hey guys!' We'd go on hikes, and she'd be there. She was always around."

What infuriated agents is that Snow seemed to think he was successfully pulling the wool over their eyes.

In commenting, Cullen said neither Snow nor his family "improperly used the services of the U.S. Secret Service detail assigned to him. The Secret Service is required to protect the secretary of the treasury," Cullen said. "Protection is mandatory. It is not discretionary. Nor is it assigned on the basis of a threat assessment for a particular event or trip."

Snow considers Secret Service agents "professional, brave, and extremely hard-working," Cullen said. While Snow is "surprised and saddened that a former Secret Service agent would be a source of any information — particularly anonymous, erroneous information — going into a book, he believes that the honor and historic tradition of the Secret Service will remain intact, and he recalls with great fondness and affection the brave members of his detail." In view of that, Cullen said, Snow is "surprised that you would imply in your book that he had asked or demanded that his detail ever deviate from their proper role."

In fact, while Snow's lawyer is correct in

saying that the treasury secretary, along with others in the line of succession to the presidency, is required to have Secret Service protection when the secretary of homeland security authorizes it, he is wrong in saying that this book suggests that Snow asked that his detail deviate from their proper role.

The Secret Service is required to provide protection when a government official such as Snow chooses to travel from Washington every weekend, whether to see his mistress, his wife, or a play. The question is whether government officials should be taking such frequent personal trips when American taxpayers are footing the bill.

24
EXPOSING ROMNEY TO DANGER

Deciding when to protect a presidential candidate is a cat-and-mouse game. Some candidates want protection simply because it gives them more credibility as a contender and makes their lives easier. Others shun protection even when they become viable candidates and have received threats.

By law, the Secret Service provides protection of major presidential and vice presidential candidates and their spouses. The secretary of homeland security determines who the major candidates are after consulting with an advisory committee consisting of the speaker and minority leader of the House and the majority and minority leaders of the Senate, who select one additional member.

The secretary of homeland security decides when to initiate protection. Protection of spouses starts 120 days before the general election, unless the DHS or an executive order authorizes it sooner. To protect a presidential candidate, the Secret Service spends an extra $38,000 a day beyond agents' regular salaries. That includes airline tickets for agents and for advance personnel, rental cars, meals, and overtime.

Especially during campaigns, the Secret Service's dual roles of providing protection and investigating financial crimes complement each other. Agents pursuing financial crimes gain investigative experience and forge partnerships with local law enforcement. That comes in handy when agents engage in protection. At the same time, when presidential campaigns begin, the agency can pull agents from investigating financial crimes to protect candidates. In man-hours, slightly more than half of agents' time is devoted to protection.

While Barack Obama never received a specific threat before his protection started on May 3, 2007, agents on the Secret Service's Internet Threat Desk homed in on a number of vaguely threatening and nasty comments, mostly directed at the fact that he is African-American.

In the end, according to Steven Hughes, who was then deputy special agent in charge of the Dignitary Protection Division, "we really picked him up because he asked for the protection, and then it goes through a whole process of whether we will protect him or not, and it's really not driven by the Secret Service. It's something that he asked for, and the secretary of homeland security and the president ultimately said he is a viable candidate, and it's a go for protection."

Mitt Romney began receiving Secret Service protection on the evening of February 1, 2012. For four months before that, Romney paid for his own private protection from U.S. Safety and Security, headed by former Secret Service agent Joseph Funk.

As with any candidate, top Secret Service officials met with Mitt and Ann Romney to discuss protection. By then, Romney was receiving about one threat a day, mainly by letter or phone. In fact, a day before the Secret Service picked up protection, as Romney walked to the stage inside a warehouse in Eagan, Minnesota, a gay rights activist who said he represented the group Glitterati and Occupy Minneapolis threw a cup of glitter on Romney. The glitter poured over Romney's hair, stuck to his face, and shimmered from his navy blazer. Local police escorted the man out.

A week after Secret Service protection began, Peter Smith, a twenty-year-old college student, tossed a handful of blue glitter at Romney as the former Massachusetts governor was shaking hands with supporters in Denver. At the time, Smith was interning for the Democratic-controlled state senate in Colorado. He was fired after the incident and later pleaded guilty to a charge of disturbing the peace.

"We made the request to ask them to provide protection," says a high-ranking Romney campaign staffer. "We were not eager to get it. Mitt had the financial means to provide his own security. We also understood the drawbacks of Secret Service protection. We felt it created a distance between a candidate and the voters that we were not eager to have. But there were threats almost daily, and our security company said it was getting to the point where they could not guarantee his safety."

The fifteen Secret Service agents on Romney's detail found that the Romneys treated them like family. Although the agents usually declined, the Romneys invited them to lunch and dinner. Romney would kibitz with them and with the additional agents on Ann's detail. When a female agent brought her young son to a debate at Hofstra University, Romney took him aside and discussed government and politics with him.

On August 29, 2012, a female agent accidentally left her gun in the bathroom of Romney's campaign plane on a flight from Florida to Indiana. An Associated Press reporter discovered the weapon and decided to write about the incident. As a result, the Secret Service removed the agent, who had been assigned to act as liaison with the press corps, from the campaign. Romney and his aides were distressed.

"The gun was left unattended accidentally for it sounds like less than a minute, and the AP found it," a Romney aide says. "This woman was the dedicated press agent, so this woman lives with the press and spent all day every day helping them and giving them updates. A few reporters repaid her kindness and flexibility by having a meeting, and they decided that since two or three of the press corps couldn't seem to leave it alone, and they didn't want to get scooped on this non-story, several of them would write it. So the woman was transferred off of her post because of her mistake. Governor Romney was on her side and requested that she not be moved out."

In fact, Romney made the request personally to Director Mark Sullivan. But the Secret Service has a policy of not acceding to such personal requests by protectees, because allowing protectees to intervene in personnel matters would tend to undermine management and possibly weaken protection.

On election night, when Romney called Obama from his suite at the Westin Waterfront Hotel in Boston to concede that the president had won, "one of the agents was in tears," a Romney campaign aide recalls. "He was so sad that he lost. The agents became part of the family."

The next morning, before the agents departed, Ann Romney made buttermilk pancakes, which Mitt served them on paper plates in their vehicles outside the Romneys' townhome in Belmont, Massachusetts.

As is common with all campaigns, the Secret Service and Romney campaign aides engaged in a constant negotiating process that sometimes led to friction. Campaigns want the candidate accessible to supporters, while agents want fans kept at bay.

If fifty or more people were to attend an event, the Secret Service wanted to create a physical buffer between them and Romney. Romney aides wanted the partition to be a rope line. The Secret Service wanted to employ bike racks. Romney aides wanted the campaign plane to be fueled immediately as Romney's plane landed and he gave a speech at the airport. The Secret Service did not want airport personnel near the plane until they could be passed through magnetometers.

In many cases, the agents and the aides compromised: Bike racks would be set up as barriers for gatherings of a hundred people or more. Both sides understood that they were trying to do their jobs, which had competing goals. None of the issues rose to the level of importance of what had happened when the Reagan White House insisted that unscreened crowds be allowed near the president as he left the Washington Hilton.

"Typically staff wants the crowd as close as they can get to the stage," an agent says. "We obviously have to have enough of a buffer there to make it safe to move around. A good starting point is ten feet. But staff always wants to push it in, and unfortunately for us, we have management that folds to staff and doesn't articulate why we need this for security reasons. They always end up giving back some and shrinking it back to eight feet."

Despite the friction, the Romney aides came to admire agents for their professionalism. But what the aides could not understand was the refusal of Secret Service headquarters to provide enough magnetometers at events. As a result, especially during the last three months of the campaign, Romney would give a separate speech to those who were outside events and had not been passed through magnetometers, jeopardizing his safety just as surely as Reagan's safety was jeopardized.

"We had hour-long waits to get in because of the number of magnetometers they would provide," an aide says. "They had this wrong calculation, that four hundred fifty people go through a magnetometer in one hour. We did our own calculation and found the average number was two hundred to two hundred fifty. We would spend tremendous amounts of time arguing for more resources."

Privately, Secret Service agents confirm that the lower number is more realistic. But headquarters, always trying to save money, refused to budge to accommodate the Romney crowds. Besides prompting Romney to give speeches to unscreened crowds, the Secret Service would create what Romney chief strategist Stuart Stevens refers to as a two-tier system, allowing nonscreened crowds to sit farther away from Romney at events.

"Especially as we got bigger, the crowds started growing," Stevens says. "But there was always this problem of getting people into the event. The Secret Service went to having two tiers with people who were not screened with magnetometers. In addition, Mitt would come out and talk to the people outside who were not magged."

"Near the end, we usually had three events a day and had to do two speeches each time," an aide says. "If we had a thousand people outside and a thousand inside, the governor would say to his detail leader he was going outside. The governor would walk to the parking lot and give an impromptu speech. Of course, he'd be ticked if he had to do two speeches instead of one. But we were not going to walk out of Des Moines with mad voters. These people outside events had not been screened with magnetometers and could have had firearms."

In addition to calculating how many people actually go through a magnetometer in an hour, the Romney campaign dispatched aides to observe Obama events. Being president, Obama was provided with enough magnetometers so that most people could enter events before they started, the aides found. As a result, Obama's events came across on television as better attended.

"Basically the president's detail gets first

whack at everything, and all the other details, there's kind of a pecking order, and it's hard to say it, but they get a lesser level of protection the further down the pecking order you go," a former agent says. "There's not enough bodies to go around, not enough budget, not enough resources."

Romney aides pointed out to the Secret Service that their magnetometer calculations were off. They would argue about whether the Secret Service would provide four or six magnetometers at an event. "They would say, 'Well, this is expensive equipment that had to be flown in,' " an aide says.

As a result, a country that spent $113 million in fiscal 2012 to protect the presidential candidates would not scrape together funds to provide enough magnetometers at events held by a possible future president. The same kind of corner cutting ordered by the Reagan White House led to the shooting of President Reagan.

If Romney had been taken out by an assassin with a handgun in a parking lot or with grenades in an unscreened area of an arena, the Secret Service's failure to provide enough magnetometers would have been exposed as a shameful dereliction of duty. Like so much else about the Secret Service, that shortsightedness has remained a secret until now.

The misplaced priorities go back to an entrenched Secret Service management culture that boasts that the agency "makes do with less" and that dismisses criticism with the cavalier explanation that the Secret Service has "always done it this way."

25
INTRUSION

As a *Washington Post* reporter covering the social scene for twenty years, Roxanne Roberts thought she had seen it all — until one evening at the White House.

Covering the state dinner for Indian prime minister Manmohan Singh on Tuesday, November 24, 2009, Roberts looked up from the guest list and saw a couple who looked exactly like Michaele and Tareq Salahi. With her long blond mane, Michaele — wearing a striking red-and-gold traditional Indian *lehenga* — was hard to miss.

Going back to 2005, Roberts had been writing the *Post*'s Reliable Source gossip column with Amy Argetsinger. Over the years, they had reported on legal wrangling over the Salahis' Oasis Winery in Hume, Virginia, and on complaints that patrons had been ripped off by a polo championship the Salahis ran. More recently, Roberts and Argetsinger had written about the couple's effort to be selected for Bravo's *Real Housewives of D.C.*

"I immediately looked down at the guest list and saw that they weren't on it," Roberts recalls. "I have never in all the years covering state dinners seen a guest come through who wasn't on the list." The idea that they had not been invited did not occur to her. Rather, Roberts was shocked to think they were.

"I knew that they weren't wealthy," Roberts notes. "I knew they were not big political donors or moved in any significant political circles. They were not what I would call part of Washington's power establishment, by any stretch of the imagination."

Wanting to hear Argetsinger's opinion, Roberts asked a *Washington Post* photographer to e-mail her colleague a photo he had just taken of the Salahis.

"I recognized them, and my first reaction when I saw the photos of them was 'Oh my God, they crashed,' " Argetsinger says. "Because they are not the kind of people you expect to see at the White House. If the one thing you knew about them was that Michaele Salahi was vying to be on the *Housewives* show, it would be inconceivable that the White House would want them there. This is a reality TV show, and one that in recent years is best known for pretty vapid material — plastic surgery, catfights, table flipping, hair pulling."

Argetsinger e-mailed Rox, as she calls her, urging her to include in the story she would write with Robin Givhan that the Salahis attended but were not on the guest list.

"The most curious and unexpected sighting: Tareq and Michaele Salahi," their story said in the sixth paragraph. "The notorious Fauquier County vineyard socialites, who are filming *Real Housewives of D.C.,* swanned in, even though their names did not appear on the official guest list."

"Everyone who enters the White House grounds goes through magnetometers and several other levels of screenings," Secret Service spokesman Edwin Donovan was quoted in the article as saying. "That was the case with the state dinner last night. No one was under any risk or threat."

That is the standard Secret Service line when the agency has screwed up. What Donovan failed to say was that the Salahis had managed to enter the White House without the required background check. Normally, those attending a White House function will receive an invitation in the mail. If they are to attend, they must e-mail or call in their full name, Social Security

314

number, and date of birth. The Secret Service's Uniformed Division checks to see if they are listed by the National Crime Information Center (NCIC) or the National Law Enforcement Telecommunications System (NLETS) as having been arrested or violated laws. If no problem surfaces, invitees are told they have been cleared to attend.

None of that took place in the case of the Salahis. For all the Secret Service knew, the couple could have been wanted terrorists or serial killers. While they passed through magnetometers at the checkpoint at Fifteenth and E Streets NW, they could have had chemical or biological weapons. Inside, they could have grabbed a knife from a table and stabbed the president in the heart.

After Roberts kept pushing, the White House and Secret Service confirmed that the Salahis had not been invited. The story ran on all the networks.

On Friday, the White House released a photo of the couple in the receiving line. A smiling Michaele Salahi is pictured clasping Obama's hand, as her husband, wearing a tuxedo, looks on. Prime Minister Singh is standing next to the president.

Secret Service director Sullivan finally stepped forward and issued a statement saying the agency was "deeply concerned and embarrassed" by the incident. He said preliminary findings indicated that "established protocols were not followed at an initial checkpoint, verifying that two individuals were on the guest list."

In administrations past, aides from the White House Social Office have stood outside the Secret Service guard post, performing a preliminary check to make sure that arrivals were on the guest list. Acquiescent as always, the Secret Service this time had agreed at a meeting with the Social Office that their representatives would not have to be there. Instead, social secretary Desiree Rogers took the unusual step of attending the dinner herself as a guest.

Yet the fact that the Salahis were able to crash the White House was the fault of the Secret Service. The Secret Service is solely responsible for the security of the president and the White House. Regardless of what the Social Office did, it was up to the Secret Service uniformed officers at the first checkpoint to verify that the couple was on the guest list. If they were not, the officers should have called the Social Office to see if they had inadvertently been left off the list. If the answer was yes, the officers would then have asked the couple to step aside while they did a background check. They did none of this.

As I later reported, it turned out that a third crasher, Carlos Allen, had also been allowed into the state dinner. Weeks after the event took place, the Secret Service pinpointed him while reviewing surveillance videos of guests arriving at the dinner.

The publisher of a minor Washington society blog called *Hush Society Magazine,* Allen, thirty-nine, claimed he fell in with the India delegation congregating at the Willard Inter-Continental Hotel and rolled on in with them.

Like the Salahis, the man turned out not to pose a threat, but because the Secret Service failed to perform a background check, the agency never would have known if he was, for example, wanted for murder or involved with terrorist groups. Ironically, in the movie *In the Line of Fire,* an assassin gains access to the president in similar fashion. Like the Salahis, Carlos Allen claimed he had been invited. But the "invitation" he later showed on a television show appeared to be the dinner program for the evening, according to the *Washington Post*'s Reliable Source.

Until I reported the story on Allen, mortified Secret Service officials had failed to notify the House Homeland Security Committee investigating the Salahi security breach of yet another embarrassment to the agency. It would have made little difference, since the committee whitewashed the incident. At a hearing, the House members called as a witness only Sullivan, who rejected any notion that the intrusions were a symptom of deeper problems within the Secret Service.

Why would Secret Service Uniformed Division officers let in three individuals who were not on the guest list and had not undergone a background check? The fact that Secret Service management removed Mary Cheney's detail leader after he refused to violate the rules to allow agents to take her friends to restaurants suggests the reason.

Agents and uniformed officers say their perception is that the Secret Service's spineless management, which condones cutting corners, likely would not back them if they turned away glamorous crashers and it later came to light that they had been left off the guest list by mistake.

The same management culture contributed to Secret Service agents' engaging prostitutes while assigned to protect President Obama in Cartagena, Colombia. The saga began when agents checked into the Hotel Caribe, a beachfront resort, and decided to explore local bars and nightclubs. On the evening of Wednesday, April 11, 2012, agent Arthur Huntington, forty-one, made his way with some other agents to Tu Candela, a bar and dance club in the city's old town.

Huntington spotted the alluring Dania Suarez, who later told the *New York Times* she was not a common streetwalker. Rather, she said, she was a woman of "higher rank" whom a "man can take out to dinner. She can dress nicely, wear nice makeup, speak and act like a lady. That's me."

After dancing with the twenty-four-year-old, the married Huntington took Suarez to his hotel. On the way, she says, she stopped to buy condoms and told the agent that if he were going to spend the night with her, he would have to give her a "gift" of eight hundred dollars. He didn't object, she said.

Under hotel policy, temporary female guests must register with the front desk for a fee and must leave by 6 A.M. At 6:30 A.M. on Thursday, April 12, the front desk called Huntington to say it was time for his guest to leave. Suarez asked for her eight hundred dollars.

"I tell him, 'Baby, my cash money,' " she later said.

Claiming he did not know Suarez was a prostitute, Huntington, a member of the counterassault team, refused to pay her. Calling her a bitch, he gave the brunette thirty dollars in local currency and shoved her out the door.

Suarez was crying as she banged on the door to the room of another agent, who was sleeping with a friend of hers. He and a third agent scraped together another two hundred fifty dollars to pay her. The ensuing commotion led to the Colombian National Police being called in, the State Department being notified, and twelve agents being interrogated in Cartagena by Paula Reid, the special agent in charge of the Miami field office, which oversees activities in Colombia. On the morning of Friday, April 13, eleven of those agents were relieved of their protective duties, put on administrative leave, and sent home.

Later that afternoon, Obama arrived in Cartagena for the weekend's Summit of the Americas, a meeting of thirty-three of the hemisphere's thirty-five leaders, to discuss economic policy and trade. At about the same time, I received a call from a longtime Secret Service source. A critic of Director

Sullivan, the agent told me what had happened in Colombia and that the agents were being sent home. He said Sullivan planned to keep the incident a secret. Indeed, since it could have been seen as an internal personnel matter, the agency could plausibly have said it was obligated to keep the entire matter confidential.

While he declined to give the specific reason, Secret Service spokesman Edwin Donovan confirmed to me that agents were being sent home. I gave the story to the *Washington Post,* which jumped on it and ran the story the next day, touching off a media frenzy.

During the ensuing investigation, another Secret Service employee admitted to paying for sex at a private apartment, according to a January 2013 report by the DHS Office of Inspector General. Nearly all the agents involved lost their jobs or were forced to retire.

The scandal represented a serious breach of the rules, which are designed to prevent agents from being compromised and then blackmailed to allow access to those who may wish to harm or eavesdrop on the president. According to those rules, Secret Service employees "shall not engage in criminal, infamous, dishonest, immoral or notoriously disgraceful conduct or other conduct prejudicial to the [United States] government."

Contrary to some press reports, this kind of misconduct is not common, as confirmed by a December 17, 2013, report by the DHS inspector general. While agents may have drinks after the president has departed, hiring prostitutes is a rare occurrence. But given management's lax attitude toward security, it's easy to see how the agents figured that if their bosses cut corners, why shouldn't they ignore basic security rules as well?

26

RISKING ASSASSINATION

Today about a third of the Secret Service's annual budget goes to investigation of financial crimes like counterfeiting and fraudulently obtaining money from ATMs or checking or credit card accounts. While the Secret Service's work in solving these crimes is impressive, with the exception of counterfeit currency investigations, the FBI probes the same crimes. Yet the Secret Service has sought greater jurisdiction in going after financial crimes even as protection demands soar.

Besides having to protect more White House staff, the Secret Service is now charged with planning and implementing security arrangements at "special events of national significance" under the Presidential Threat Protection Act of 2000. The first such event was the Winter Olympics in Salt Lake City in 2002. Other events are the September meetings of the United Nations

General Assembly, presidential inaugurals, the Democratic and Republican nominating conventions, the Super Bowl, G8 summits, and major visits, such as a pope's trip to the United States. The state funerals of Presidents Reagan and Ford were also designated national special security events. At these events, the Secret Service is the lead law enforcement agency and coordinates all security.

In an apparent effort to conceal a huge increase in trips taken by President Obama and Vice President Biden compared with their predecessors, after Obama took office, the Secret Service stopped breaking out figures on their trips. But the aggregate numbers give some idea of the pressures agents face. In fiscal 2011, the Secret Service provided protection for 3,284 domestic and 376 international travel stops for Obama, Biden, and other national leaders.

As demands on the Secret Service increase, the agency fails to request a commensurate increase in funds and instead pressures agents to work long overtime hours. That has led to exhausted agents having no home life.

"We were trained to be alert and constantly on edge, yet we were forced to work a twelve-to-fourteen-hour shift, hop on a plane to another city, sleep four hours, and do it all over again," a former agent says. "We had no set schedule and could work a midnight shift one day, a day shift another, and an afternoon shift the next and have a day off on Wednesday. Even airline pilots have mandatory rest periods, but here we were standing next to the president of the United States and were expected to make split-second, life-or-death decisions."

"How tired do you get? Just imagine sleeping three or four hours a night for a week," a current agent says.

As a result of management's lack of regard for agents' quality of life, resignations before retirement have shot up in recent years. Since 9/11, the private sector has offered lucrative compensation to anyone with a federal law enforcement background. Former Secret Service agents often sign on as vice presidents for security of major corporations or start their own security firms. For those who want to remain vested to earn full government pensions, opportunities have expanded at other federal law enforcement agencies.

"These people who are leaving are very qualified agents who are doing a really good job and are held in high esteem," an agent says. "That's what really hurts us."

The Secret Service's corner cutting and mismanagement extend to polygraph testing that would detect an infiltrator. Before being hired, applicants to the Secret Service must pass a polygraph exam. But after they sign up, agents are never again required to undergo regular lie detector testing. In contrast, the FBI polygraphs all employees — not just agents — every five years. FBI counterintelligence agents are polygraphed more often.

Given the lack of polygraphing, the Secret Service leaves itself open to a terrorist organization or a foreign intelligence service recruiting an agent to provide access to the president for an assassination or to allow installation of bugging devices or access to top secret information. Regular polygraphing would likely detect such a compromise, as well as deter it.

The FBI learned the hard way the importance of regular polygraph testing. After the arrest of CIA officer Aldrich Ames in 1994 for spying, Robert "Bear" Bryant, as head of the bureau's National Security Division, urged FBI director Louis Freeh to approve regular polygraphs for all counterintelligence agents. But faced with opposition from many special agents in charge of field offices and from the FBI Agents Association, Freeh backed down and shelved the proposal.

While polygraph tests are not perfect, if nothing else they are a deterrent. If Freeh had in fact approved Bryant's proposal in 1994 to polygraph counterintelligence agents, FBI agent Robert Hanssen likely would have decided to stop spying for the Russians. Instead, for seven years after Freeh refused to allow regular polygraphing, Hanssen continued to provide the Russians with some of the most damaging information in the history of American espionage.

In addition, the FBI's nearly fourteen thousand agents are required to attend annual updates on law, ethics, and security. But after initial training, Secret Service agents receive no annual in-service instruction, and training in security is limited to a minimal update online. After the scandal involving agents hiring prostitutes in Colombia, the Secret Service announced it would provide ethics training — but only to a hundred agents.

"Local police departments have in-service training every year," says a Secret Service agent. "You are updated on basic criminal law, new court rulings, about probable cause, what you need to develop in order to detain someone. The Secret Service teaches agents once, in their basic training, and there is no training on developments after that."

Much like a car that never gets regular maintenance and oil changes, the seven-thousand-employee Secret Service lurches along until a tragedy like the Kennedy assassination forces it to rectify deficiencies. No one can rationally explain the "we make do with less" mind-set and lackadaisical attitude that prevent the Secret Service from adequately protecting presidents, vice presidents, and presidential candidates.

To let people into events without magnetometer screening, to scrimp on magnetometers to the point where Mitt Romney felt forced to deliver campaign speeches to unscreened crowds in parking lots, to bow to Joe Biden's wishes to be without the nuclear football or adequate protection in Delaware, to divert agents from protecting the president when he takes off in Marine One from the White House so they can protect the Secret Service director's assistant, to allow Bradley Cooper's vehicle into a secure restricted area without screening before Obama was to give a speech, and to disregard firearms requalification and physical fitness requirements, are each so egregious that few past government scandals are comparable because so much is at stake. Each lapse by the Secret Service directly risks the life of the president, vice president, and presidential candidates.

Yet when one such scandal became public — uniformed officers allowing party crashers into the White House state dinner — President Obama took no action to prevent such debacles in the future. Even after the Colombia prostitution scandal, Obama brushed aside the signs that the Secret Service is in need of a drastic overhaul and defended Mark Sullivan, who presided over the embarrassments as director.

When addressing the Colombia scandal, President Obama said he would be "angry" if the allegations in the press turned out to be true. But in commenting to me for the original story, the Secret Service confirmed that agents were being withdrawn for misconduct. Being angry is not the way to fix an agency. Holding management accountable is.

When Sullivan retired, Obama appointed Julia Pierson as the agency's twenty-third director, on March 27, 2013. A native of Orlando, Florida, Pierson graduated from the University of Central Florida and completed graduate course studies in public policy at George Washington University. She served as a police officer in Orlando and began her career in the Secret Service as a special agent assigned to the Miami and Orlando field offices.

During her thirty-year career with the agency, Pierson was deputy assistant director in the Office of Protective Operations, where she was responsible for daily security operations. She was also assistant director of the Office of Human Resources and Training (HRT). Most recently, she had been Sullivan's chief of staff for five years.

While agents express approval of the appointment of a female director, they say Pierson is a clone of Sullivan. She has taken no steps to rectify problems within the agency. Despite the increased risk to the president, Pierson was slow to navigate a way around the automatic budget cuts imposed on critical functions by sequestration, as other agencies like the Defense Department did by reprogramming funds. Because of the sequester, agents say vital protective work left protectees exposed to potential danger.

"Agents are exhausted trying to backfill the assignments, and morale is the lowest it's ever been," an agent says.

Pierson's response to misconduct by two supervisory agents on the President's Protective Detail is instructive. In May 2013, officials at the stately Hay-Adams Hotel in Washington alerted the Secret Service that supervisory agent Ignacio Zamora Jr. was causing a disturbance, the *Washington Post* reported. An internal investigation found that Zamora had been visiting a woman in her hotel room across from the White House. When she realized that Zamora had a weapon, she became agitated.

To reassure her, Zamora removed the bullets from his gun, but she insisted that he leave. After exiting her room, he realized that he had accidentally left one round in her room. He returned and tried to persuade her to open her door so he could retrieve the bullet, but she refused. Still, he kept trying, drawing the attention of hotel security.

In investigating the incident, the Secret Service found that both Zamora and another supervisor, Timothy Barraclough, had been sending sexually explicit e-mails on their government-issued BlackBerrys to a female subordinate. What has not come out previously is that Director Pierson signed off on reassigning Zamora to a supervisory position in the Protective Intelligence and

Assessment Division, and on transferring Barraclough to head the Tucson resident office. Agents see the moves as a continuation of the double standard applied to supervisors versus agents.

"Zamora got a lateral transfer, same position, same title in another division," an agent says. "So there's no punishment there. He is still an assistant special agent in charge. Barraclough was assistant to the special agent in charge and was given what is considered a promotion at the same salary level to be in charge of his own resident office. The guy suffered nothing — no demotion, no punishment."

While subordinates are punished severely on a regular basis, "bosses are not," the agent says. "The problem of agent misconduct is caused by managers who do the same things themselves and are not held accountable for it."

In a round of talks to agents, Pierson acknowledged that turnover has been increasing and said she would work on some salary issues. But she made no mention of the lax management culture that has led to corner cutting.

Confirming that Pierson learned nothing from the agency's past mistakes, the Secret Service under her watch failed to warn

President Obama to forgo speaking at Nelson Mandela's memorial service in South Africa on December 10, 2013, because local authorities were letting in spectators without any magnetometer screening. It was a repeat of how local authorities failed to screen crowds when President George W. Bush spoke in Tbilisi, Georgia, in 2005, allowing a man to throw a grenade at him.

"I was shocked at the apparent lack of any real security measures, precautions, or deterrents," reporter Scott Thuman of Washington television station WJLA told Politico. "We entered the stadium along with a steady but manageable crowd of people through the main gates, which were completely unattended. There were no workers performing bag checks or patdowns — there were no magnetometers to walk through, no metal detector wands being used — anywhere."

One of those not screened was bogus sign language interpreter Thamsanqa Jantjie, who stood three feet from Obama and other world leaders during the service at Soweto's FNB stadium. In 2003, Jantjie was part of a group that accosted two men found with a stolen television and burned them to death by setting fire to tires placed around their necks. As a result of the murders, Jantjie was institutionalized for at least a year. Yet in commenting on that fact, Secret Service spokesman Donovan covered up the obvious security lapses by saying "agreed-upon security measures between the U.S. Secret Service and South African government security officials were in place" during the service. He thus implicitly confirmed that the Secret Service had failed to warn Obama of the security breakdown so that he could decide whether to appear at the event or address the crowds remotely by television.

"I really don't think the president should be going to these sorts of events unless there's some guarantee that the domestic security force has a plan that's operational and workable," says former agent Dan Bongino, who was on George W. Bush's protective detail.

Reflecting her priorities, just after taking office, Pierson sent an e-mail to all agents reminding them to maintain a "professional appearance." Tattoos should not be visible, and facial hair must be short and "neatly groomed," she instructed. The FBI under J. Edgar Hoover reflected the same obsession with image, helping to conceal the bureau's many flaws.

Pierson may have done nothing to reform

the agency, but she loves taking trips with Obama on Air Force One, as she did when Obama flew to the Netherlands in March 2014. There, three agents who were assigned to protect the president were sent home for misconduct after a night of drinking. Hotel personnel found one of the agents passed out in a hallway. While the agents obviously lacked any common sense, their punishment reflected the agency's continuing double standard: Agents in the field may suffer severe repercussions for transgressions, while management orders agents to take risks that could result in an assassination.

The Secret Service's annual budget is $1.6 billion — about half the cost of one B-2 Stealth Bomber. Given the importance of the presidency, doubling that figure would be money well spent. But rather than request substantially more funds, the Secret Service assures President Obama and members of Congress that the agency is fulfilling its job with the modest increases it requests, even as it takes on more duties, and sleep-deprived agents work almost around the clock. Yet scrimping on protection of the president, the vice president, and presidential candidates risks an assassination that would undermine American democracy.

If the Secret Service has fallen down on its duties, it is unexcelled at providing special access to members of Congress and sweet-talking them, the media, and the president into thinking that it is competent. That is one reason the press never questioned why the Secret Service would allow John Hinckley to get within fifteen feet of President Reagan as he left the Washington Hilton. Like Hoover's FBI, which dishonestly padded arrest statistics, just as the Secret Service does by taking credit for arrests made by local police, the USSS skillfully projects a rosy image it does not deserve.

Only an outside director with a fresh perspective — as Robert S. Mueller III had when he took over as FBI director — would be capable of reforming Secret Service management and changing the culture that fosters corner cutting and punishes agents who question it. Unlike former FBI director Freeh, who dissed anyone who brought him bad news, Mueller removed FBI officials who did not level with him.

Obama's failure to heed the warning signs is as reckless as President Kennedy's refusal to let agents ride on the rear running board of his limousine in Dallas or the insistence of the staff of the Reagan White House that unscreened members of the public be allowed close to President Reagan as he left the Washington Hilton. Yet Congress has also been derelict in its duty. When it comes to selecting a Secret Service director, Congress has never demanded accountability by requiring Senate confirmation.

The list of positions that do require Senate confirmation is long and the positions often obscure. Not only the head of the U.S. Marshals Service requires Senate confirmation but also ninety-four marshals positions, one in each judicial district. Besides the head of the Drug Enforcement Agency, the director of the Justice Department's Office for Victims of Crime requires confirmation. So does the librarian of Congress and the deputy director for demand reduction of the so-called drug czar. The Secret Service director is missing from this list.

Yet along with the FBI, whose director does require confirmation, the Secret Service is the paramount agency responsible for protecting American democracy. And given its powers, the service's potential for engaging in abuses is almost as great as the FBI's.

In imposing greater accountability, Secret Service agents should be required to report to the director in writing any instruction to ignore the agency's security recommenda-tions — whether it comes from Secret Service supervisors, the president, the vice president, a presidential candidate, or their staffs. While a protectee is free to override Secret Service recommendations, the Secret Service director would then be held respon-sible if he or she did not take steps to persuade the individual to adhere to Secret Service advice.

In the case of protectees' staffs or Secret Service supervisors, the director would be responsible for failing to tell agents to disregard requests that undercut security. If that simple solution had been in effect when the Reagan White House pressured Secret Service agents to let unscreened members of the public approach President Reagan, Hinckley never could have shot him.

Entering Secret Service headquarters, you see on the wall the words "Worthy of Trust and Confidence" in big silver letters. Since the Secret Service first began protecting presidents, that has been an admonishment to agents not to reveal what they see behind the scenes. After I broke the story of agents' engaging prostitutes in Cartagena, the Secret Service reinforced that dictate by requiring agents to sign confidentiality agreements, suggesting by the timing a desire to avoid future embarrassment.

On the surface, it may seem to be a legitimate point that if agents are not discreet, protectees may not trust them and therefore may want to evade them if the protectees choose to engage in embarrassing activities. But the American people also legitimately have a right to know about the true character of their leaders. Often, Secret Service agents are the only ones who see what those in the White House are really like. Like human surveillance cameras, Secret Service agents are uniquely positioned to assess a president's character.

Those who run for high office should expect a high degree of scrutiny and to be held accountable for personal indiscretions that conflict with their public image and reveal hypocrisy. Rather than expecting the Secret Service to cover up for them, they should not enter public life if they insist on leading double lives. That is particularly true when one considers that a president or vice president having an affair opens himself up to possible manipulation and blackmail.

"If you want the job, then you need to lead the kind of life and be the kind of person that can stand up to the scrutiny that comes with that job," says former Secret Service agent Clark Larsen.

John Adams, the second U.S. president, said the people "have a right, an indisputable, unalienable, indefeasible, divine right to that most dreaded and envied kind of knowledge — I mean of the character and conduct of their rulers."

In training new agents, the FBI Academy teaches that the best predictor of future behavior is past behavior. Yet over and over, voters have ignored warning signs of poor character and candidates' track records and focused instead on their promises, their celebrity, and their acting ability on television. It's a blindness that they would never extend to choosing a friend, a new employee, an electrician, or a plumber. Yet in entrusting the country and their security to a president, they are making a far more important decision.

Each time, voters have regretted disregarding those clues to character. When running for vice president, Richard Nixon became embroiled in an ethics issue when the *New York Post* revealed he had secretly accepted $18,000 from private contributors to defray his expenses, an issue Nixon addressed in what became known as his Checkers speech. It should have come as no surprise that Nixon ended up driven from office by the scandal known as Watergate.

Almost as if they feel undeserving of honorable, trustworthy politicians, Americans too often fall for the phony argument that so long as they do not influence public acts, flaws in a candidate's character are nobody's business. But human beings do not consist of two spheres, public and private. Poor judgment, hypocrisy, ruthlessness, deceit, arrogance, and corruption displayed in one's personal life inevitably manifest themselves in public life.

Character is who we are. To disregard that is to court disaster. Once a candidate becomes president, any character flaws are magnified. It is difficult to imagine the pressure that being president of the United States imposes and how readily the power of being president corrupts. To be in command of the most powerful country on earth, to be able to fly anywhere at a moment's notice on Air Force One, to take action that affects millions of lives is an intoxicating experience that only people with the most stable personalities and solid values can handle. Inviting a friend to a White House party or having an assistant place a call and announce that "the White House is calling" has such a potent effect on people that presidents and White House aides come to believe that, like Superman, they are invincible.

"I would see CEOs make asses of themselves trying to ingratiate themselves with presidents," a former agent says. "They revert back to fourth graders. They stumble over their words. They flush with embarrassment. It never fails."

"Their egos get so big they can't believe anybody could tell them what to do, and they can't control themselves," former agent Richard Repasky says of presidents.

Trivial though it may seem, even the use of the honorific "Mr. President" leads some who have held that office to think they are divine.

"Few people, with the possible exception of his wife, will ever tell a president that he is a fool," President Ford lamented in his book, *A Time to Heal.* "There's a majesty to the office that inhibits even your closest friends from saying what is really on their minds. They won't tell you that you just made a lousy speech or bungled a chance to get your point across. Instead, they'll say they liked the speech you gave last week a little better or that an even finer opportunity to get your point across will come very soon. You can tell them you want the blunt truth; you can leave instructions on every bulletin board, but the guarded response you get never varies."

Disillusioned by President Johnson's arrogance, his press secretary George Reedy brilliantly analyzed how presidents become consumed by the office in his book *The Twilight of the Presidency.* "The atmosphere of the White House is a heady one," Reedy warned. "By the twentieth century, the presidency had taken on all the regalia of monarchy except robes, a scepter, and a crown."

"The White House is a character crucible," says Bertram S. Brown, M.D., a psychiatrist who formerly headed the National Institute of Mental Health and was an aide to President Kennedy. "It either creates or distorts character. Few decent people want to subject themselves to the kind of grueling abuse candidates take when they run in the first place," says Dr. Brown, who has seen in his practice many top Washington politicians and White House aides. "Many of those who run crave superficial celebrity. They are hollow people who have no principles and simply want to be elected. Even if an individual is balanced, once someone becomes president, how does one solve the conundrum of staying real and somewhat humble when one is surrounded by the most powerful office in the land, and from becoming overwhelmed by an at times pathological environment that treats you every day as an emperor? Here is where the true strength of the character of the person, not his past accomplishments, will determine whether his presidency ends in accomplishment or failure."

Thus, unless a president comes to the office with strong character, the crushing force of the office and the adulation the chief executive receives will inevitably lead at best to poor judgment and at worst to catastrophe. As one example, the contrast between Hillary Clinton's nastiness in private and her Cheshire cat smile in public demonstrate both hypocrisy and an unbalanced personality.

The fact that Hillary fired a White House usher who was the father of four children for trying to help a former first lady with her computer and denounced and humiliated her friend Vince Foster in front of White House colleagues demonstrates Nixonian ruthlessness, hypocrisy, and paranoia that could be expected to balloon if she were ever president. Likewise, her calculated determination to overlook her husband's philandering to enhance her political fortunes suggests overweening ambition that could spiral out of control in the White

House. Nor is Hillary's nastiness with Secret Service agents — earning her a reputation as the most detested protectee — a sign of a stable individual who cares about the little people she claims to champion. Instead, agents say the real Hillary Clinton hungers for power and bears little resemblance to the image she seeks to project.

By the same token, Republican presidential candidate Newt Gingrich betrayed his true character when he showed up at the hospital bed of his first wife, Jackie, after her cancer surgeries and tried to discuss details of the divorce he wanted. Gingrich later dismissed what happened by saying the couple "got into an argument, which I think people who have gone through divorces can probably identify with."

In contrast to their professed distaste for government waste, possible Republican presidential candidates Senator Ted Cruz and Senator Rand Paul show up for five-minute interviews at Fox News with five or six fawning aides in tow. Normally, one or two aides accompany members of Congress for such appearances.

Much as Nixon's Checkers episode was an early clue to his character, Joe Biden's irresponsibility and colossal lack of judgment in refusing to let the nuclear football near him in Delaware, and his hypocrisy and arrogance in claiming to be the sheriff who cuts government waste while incurring costs of a million dollars for personal trips on Air Force Two, are early signs of potential disaster were he to become president.

"If the general public knew what was really going on inside the White House, they would scream," a former agent says. "Americans have such an idealized notion of the presidency and the virtues that go with it, honesty and so forth. That's the furthest thing from the truth." He adds, "You just shake your head when you think of all the things you've heard and seen and the faith that people have in these celebrity-type people. They are probably worse than most average individuals. . . . If we would pay attention to their track records, it's all there. We seem to put blinders on ourselves and overlook these frailties."

"No man can climb out beyond the limitations of his own character," John Morley, the British statesman, said.

Regardless of the character flaws they may see, Secret Service agents are sworn to protect the president at risk to their own lives. FBI agents tend to admire Secret Service agents more than they do any other law enforcement officers. As former FBI director Mueller has told me, the Secret Service's mission of preventing a criminal act is "far harder than investigating one after it takes place."

"The Secret Service attracts a lot of people who have a code of ethics that entails self-sacrifice," Norm Jarvis, a former USSS special agent in charge, says. "These are people who are willing to sacrifice their own lives, not in a conscious way, but based on their training and culture. When they hear a gunshot, they go to an instinct mode to save the president's life."

"I think that deep down inside every agent's heart, he or she would probably imagine himself or herself being the one who could take a bullet for the president and would be so honored to be that guy," a current agent says. "I would love to be the agent who did that, and I think most of the agents that I know would feel that way. It's out of our own sense of personal pride and dignity."

If agents often feel underappreciated and abused, there are compensations. Former agent Patrick Sullivan recalls returning to Washington on Air Force One after four reelection campaign stops across the country for President George H. W. Bush.

"It was ten o'clock at night when we're all sitting on Air Force One on our way back," Sullivan says. "We were complaining about the long day, and our shift leader looked at us and said, 'You know, those people who got their picture taken with him paid some ungodly amount of money just to stand next to him and get their picture taken. Do you know what they'd pay to be in that seat that you're in right now?' "

Brave and dedicated though they are, Secret Service agents' management has let them down, risking an assassination.

"We don't have enough people or the equipment to do protection the way they advertise they do," a veteran agent says. "And how we have not had an incident up to this point is truly amazing — a miracle."

SECRET SERVICE
CHRONOLOGY

1865 The Secret Service Division is created on July 5 in Washington, D.C., to suppress counterfeit currency. Chief William P. Wood is sworn in by Treasury Secretary Hugh McCulloch.

1867 Secret Service responsibilities are broadened to include "detecting persons perpetrating frauds against the government." The Secret Service begins investigating the Ku Klux Klan, nonconforming distillers, smugglers, mail robbers, perpetrators of land fraud, and other violators of federal laws.

1870 Secret Service headquarters relocates to New York City.

1874 Secret Service headquarters returns to Washington, D.C.

1875 The first commission book and a new badge are issued to operatives.

1877 Congress passes an act prohibiting the

counterfeiting of any coin or gold or silver bar.

1883 The Secret Service is officially acknowledged as a distinct organization within the Treasury Department.

1894 The Secret Service begins informal, part-time protection of President Grover Cleveland.

1901 Congress informally requests Secret Service protection of presidents following the assassination of President William McKinley.

1902 The Secret Service assumes full-time responsibility for protection of the president. Two operatives are assigned to the White House detail.

1906 Congress passes the Sundry Civil Expenses Act for 1907, providing funds for Secret Service protection of the president. Secret Service operatives begin to investigate western land frauds.

1908 The Secret Service begins protecting the president-elect. President Theodore Roosevelt transfers some Secret Service agents to the Department of Justice, forming the nucleus of what is now the Federal Bureau of Investigation.

1913 Congress authorizes permanent protection of the president and the president-elect.

1915 President Woodrow Wilson directs the secretary of the treasury to have the Secret Service investigate espionage in the United States.

1917 Congress authorizes permanent protection of the president's immediate family and makes it a federal criminal violation to direct threats toward the president.

1922 The White House Police Force is created at the request of President Warren Harding.

1930 The White House Police Force is placed under the supervision of the Secret Service.

1951 Congress enacts legislation that permanently authorizes Secret Service protection of the president, his immediate family, the president-elect, and the vice president if he requests it.

1961 Congress authorizes protection of former presidents for a reasonable period of time.

1962 Congress expands protection to include the vice president, the vice president-elect, and the next officer in line to succeed the president. Under current law, their immediate families receive protection as well. Such protection may not be declined.

1965 Congress makes assassinating a president a federal crime. It authorizes the protection of former presidents and their spouses for life and of their children until age sixteen.

1968 As a result of Robert F. Kennedy's assassination, Congress authorizes protection of major presidential and vice presidential candidates and nominees. Congress also authorizes protection of widows of presidents until death or remarriage.

1970 The White House Police Force is renamed the Executive Protective Service and given increased responsibilities, including protection of diplomatic missions in the Washington area.

1971 Congress authorizes Secret Service protection for visiting heads of foreign states or governments, and other official guests, as directed by the president.

1975 The duties of the Executive Protective Service are expanded to include protection of foreign diplomatic missions located throughout the United States and its territories.

1977 The Executive Protective Service is renamed the Secret Service Uniformed Division.

1984 Congress enacts legislation making the fraudulent use of credit and debit cards a federal violation. The law authorizes the Secret Service to investigate violations relating to credit and debit card fraud, federally related computer fraud, and fraudulent identification documents.

1986 The Treasury Police Force is merged into the Secret Service Uniformed Division. A presidential directive authorizes protection of the accompanying spouse of the head of a foreign state or government.

1990 The Secret Service receives concurrent jurisdiction with Department of Justice law enforcement personnel to conduct any kind of investigation, civil or criminal, related to federally insured financial institutions.

1994 The 1994 Crime Bill is passed, providing that any person manufacturing, trafficking in, or possessing counterfeit U.S. currency abroad may be prosecuted as though the activity occurred within the United States.

1998 Broadening the jurisdiction of the Secret Service and other federal law enforcement agencies, the Telemarketing Fraud Prevention Act allows for criminal forfeiture of the proceeds of fraud. The Identity Theft and Assumption Deterrence Act establishes the offense of identity theft. Penalties are established for anyone who knowingly transfers or uses, without authority, any means of identification of another person with the intent to commit an unlawful activity.

2000 The Presidential Threat Protection Act authorizes the Secret Service to participate in the planning, coordination, and implementation of security operations at special events of national significance as determined by the president. These events are called national special security events.

2001 The Patriot Act expands the Secret Service's role in investigating fraud and related activity in connection with computers.

2002 The Department of Homeland Security is established, taking over the Secret Service from the Department of the Treasury effective March 1, 2003.

2006 Mark Sullivan, who joined the Secret Service in 1983, is named director.

2007 Protection begins for presidential candidate Barack Obama on May 3, the earliest initiation of Secret Service protection for any candidate in U.S. history. Because of her status as a former first lady, presidential candidate Hillary Clinton was already receiving protection before she entered the race.

2008 Protection of presidential candidate

John McCain begins on April 27. Just before the presidential candidates announce their selections for vice presidential running mates, Joe Biden and Sarah Palin receive protection. After Obama is elected president on November 4, his children, Malia and Sasha, receive Secret Service protection.

2009 Barack Obama is sworn in as the forty-fourth president on January 20.

On November 24, the Secret Service allows Michaele and Tareq Salahi into a White House state dinner even though they are not on the guest list and did not undergo a background check. Subsequently, the Secret Service finds that a third intruder, Carlos Allen, attended the dinner.

2012 Republican presidential candidate Mitt Romney begins receiving Secret Service protection on January 4.

After local police are called when a Secret Service agent assigned to protect President Obama during his trip to Cartagena, Colombia, refused to pay a prostitute her agreed-upon fee, the Secret Service sends home eleven agents believed to have engaged prostitutes. The author breaks the story in the *Washington Post* on April 14.

2013 President Obama signs legislation on January 10 granting lifetime Secret Service protection to all former presidents and their spouses. The Former Presidents Protection Act reverses a 1994 law that said that after January 1, 1997, former presidents were to be protected for only ten years after leaving office. As a result of the reversal, Obama and George W. Bush and their spouses will receive lifetime protection.

Julia Pierson is sworn in as the twenty-third director of the United States Secret Service in an Oval Office ceremony on March 27. A thirty-year veteran of the agency, Pierson had been chief of staff to Director Mark Sullivan.

ACKNOWLEDGMENTS

With my twentieth book, it seems appropriate to reflect on the person who made it all possible, my wife, Pamela Kessler. Back in 1985, Pam strongly supported my risky decision to leave the *Washington Post* and write books.

A former *Washington Post* reporter and author of *Undercover Washington: Where Famous Spies Lived, Worked, and Loved*, Pam pre-edits my book manuscripts, accompanies me on visits to sites such as the Secret Service training center to write vivid descriptions, and shares her wise judgment throughout. My partner in writing books, she is the love of my life.

My children, Greg Kessler, a New York artist, and Rachel Kessler, an independent New York public relations consultant, are a source of pride and support. My stepson, Mike Whitehead, is an endearing part of that team.

Robert Gottlieb, chairman of Trident Media Group, has been my literary agent since 1991 and has been a source of support, great ideas, and friendship.

I am fortunate to have Mary Choteborsky as my editor on this book and to have had her as my editor on my three previous books. I value her brilliant editing suggestions and astute publishing judgment.

The current and former Secret Service agents who contributed to this book did a service by informing the public about the true character of our presidents and vice presidents, about their own courageous work as agents, and about the risk to themselves and to presidents and vice presidents posed by Secret Service management's practice of undercutting protection by cutting corners.

ABOUT THE AUTHOR

Ronald Kessler is the *New York Times* bestselling author of *The Secrets of the FBI, In the President's Secret Service,* and *The CIA at War.* A former *Wall Street Journal* and *Washington Post* investigative reporter, Kessler has won eighteen journalism awards, including two George Polk awards, one for national reporting and one for community service. He was named a Washingtonian of the Year by *Washingtonian* magazine. Kessler lives in Potomac, Maryland, with his wife, Pamela Kessler.

www.RonaldKessler.com